Business Writing
Makeovers

Also by the Author
Writing That Means Business (nonfiction)
Secret Choices (novel)
Together (novel)
Holding Patterns (novel)
Young Filmmakers (nonfiction)
written with Rodger Larson

Business Writing
Makeovers

Shortcut Solutions
to Improve Your
Letters, E-Mails, and Faxes

By
Hawley Roddick

Adams Media Corporation
Avon, Massachusetts

Published by Adams Media Corporation
57 Littlefield Street, Avon, MA 02322. U.S.A.
www.adamsmedia.com

ISBN: 1-58062-768-4

Printed in Canada.

J I H G F E D C B A

Library of Congress Cataloging-in-Publication Data
Roddick, Hawley.
Business writing makeovers / by Hawley Roddick.
p. cm.
Includes index.
ISBN 1-58062-768-4
1. Business writing. I. Title.
HF5718.3 .R63 2002
808'.06665--dc21

2002009816

This publication is designed to provide accurate and authoritative information
with regard to the subject matter covered. It is sold with the understanding that
the publisher is not engaged in rendering legal, accounting, or other professional advice. If legal advice or other expert assistance is required, the services
of a competent professional person should be sought.
— From a Declaration of Principles jointly adopted by a Committee of the
American Bar Association and a Committee of Publishers and Associations

This book is available at quantity discounts for bulk purchases.
For information, call 1-800-872-5627.

Contents

TWO Provide Information 75

Inside the Organization: Announcements and Notices

Clients, Customers, and Others: Announcements and Notices

Short Reports

THREE Cultivate or Give Support 147

Inside the Organization

Clients, Customers, and Others

Acknowledgments

Executive editor Claire Gerus suggested makeovers as a theme for this book, and she is the ideal editor for it because she has given workshops in corporate writing skills. And Michael Snell, my agent, exemplifies good-humored expertise.

For sharing their knowledge with me in areas beyond my own competence, I am grateful to my sister, Elizabeth Roddick Hardy; her husband, Ronald Hardy; my son, Luke Meade; and my long-time friend, Marshall Matson. Many thanks, also, to Mike Rogers for referring me to Web sites that present a quick course in technical jargon.

In addition, I appreciate the exchanges with participants in my corporate writing workshops and private coaching sessions. These people expanded my acquaintance with the business world. Finally, a tip of the hat to clients who provide business writing and editing assignments that offer an additional benefit of allowing me close-up views of their interesting professions.

Introduction

At the office, do you ever feel you have to choose between writing well and writing fast—between achieving maximum effectiveness and getting the writing task out of the way so you can move on to the next item on your to-do list? This book, by addressing that double bind, will help you write for results in a minimum amount of time.

Innovative Format

The book contains four chapters that cover the four major reasons for writing in business (two or more of these goals are often combined): to get or take *action*, to provide *information*, to cultivate or give *support*, and to promote *goodwill*. In every chapter, you will find before and after examples. Each of the 93 sets of examples contains an Original, a Formula, a Makeover, and a Checklist.

Original

The Original is a typical business letter, memo, fax, or e-mail. Topics are familiar—a cover letter for a résumé, a request for a proposal, a suggestion to a client, a defense of price increases, and so on.

The Formula

As a guide for organizing your ideas, the Formula can be adapted to a variety of situations. Here is the Formula for requesting a raise:

Beginning: State (a) your job title, (b) how long you have been in that position, (c) how long you have been with the organization, (d) what raise you seek, and (e) what your salary or wages would be after the raise.

Middle: Supply convincing evidence that you deserve a raise now; mention any commendations from those inside and outside your organization.

End: Affirm that you like working for the company (if you do) and are good at your job; repeat the amount of the raise you request.

Makeover

In a Makeover, you factor in the reader's point of view; prioritize ideas; fine-tune your language; and telegraph your main points to the reader through astute use of headings, lists, indented sentences, short paragraphs, boldface, and italics. And although Originals and Makeovers are placed against a gray background in this book, be sure to use white or ivory stationery when you write at the office.

Checklist

The Checklist tells you what improvements in the Original are needed in the Makeover. It also gives advice that applies to business correspondence in general, such as—

✓ Hyphenate a compound adjective modifying a noun, for example, *ground-based training*. But don't hyphenate adverb modifiers, which often end in *-ly—highly effective training.*
✓ Remember that *transpire* means *come to light, be revealed*. It doesn't mean *happen*.
✓ Shun indecisive words such as *perhaps* and *probably*, which create doubt in the reader's mind.

Alert readers will notice that an error in an Original may not be on the Checklist but is eliminated in the Makeover. Similarly, an error may be corrected on the Checklist, but the correction does not appear in the Makeover due to other revisions.

Resources

At the back of the book, in Resources, you will find additional tools to help you take shortcuts while writing successfully. There are checklists, tips on organization, and a one-minute grammar review.

Background for This Book

In 1984, after my book *Writing That Means Business* was published, I presented corporate writing workshops. The information in *Business Writing Makeovers* comes from the content of those workshops, their overheads and handouts—which were based on the 1984 book—and from the constant updating of business practices that I gained through immersion in my clients' organizational cultures. The situations portrayed in Originals and Makeovers are inspired by these experiences but do not depict actual people or organizations. In fact, because I also write fiction, I thought of each set of circumstances as a mini short story.

How to Use This Book

Reading and using this book is, in a sense, comparable to taking a corporate writing workshop. But the time you devote to a Makeover should depend not only on how much improvement you think the Original can benefit from but also on how important you think the letter, memo, fax, or e-mail is. Sometimes, all that is required is to quickly redesign the *look* of the Original for high impact—to make your ideas more accessible to readers.

To find the model for what you need to write, locate your topic (or a similar one) in the Contents or Index; read the Original, Formula, Makeover, and Checklist; and then either adapt the Makeover to your situation or follow the Formula and Checklist as you write.

These solutions are quick and easy. The preliminary work has been done for you, giving you timesaving shortcuts. The more you use this book, the more accustomed you will be to Makeover principles—until applying them comes naturally, and your originals may need only tinkering. That's all there is to it!

ONE
Get or Take Action

The Job

Inside the Organization

Clients, Customers, and Others

The Job

The Original

To Whom It May Concern:

I saw your ad for a collector for your credit card accounts in the "Post Examiner" and would like to interview for the job. My resume is enclosed. I hope you agree that my qualifications and references make me a strong candidate for this entry level position. Thank-you for your consideration.

Sincerely,

Emily Tower

Emily Tower

The Formula

Beginning: State what position you are applying for and mention your attached résumé.

Middle: Although you haven't had much experience, state concisely whatever qualifications make you a good candidate for the job. If you are applying for your first job after graduation from high school or college, include your grade point average and any relevant courses you have taken.

End: Close on a positive but not pushy note. If the ad gives a telephone number and does not instruct applicants not to call, say when you will follow up with a telephone call.

The Makeover

To the Tri-State Bank Human Resources Department:

You will see on my attached résumé that my qualifications closely match those you list for an entry-level collector to work with your credit card customers.

I have almost a year's experience in collections and am accustomed to working nights and weekends. My keyboarding and communication skills are strong. But my current employer does not offer the opportunities for advancement that Tri-State Bank does.

I can make a solid contribution at Tri-State as a collector and look forward to hearing from you.

Sincerely,

Emily Tower

Emily Tower

Checklist

✓ Apply ego check. Try to start with *you* not *I*.

✓ Mention the publication in which you saw the ad only if, for example, it is a professional journal and the fact that you read it enhances your image. And if you do mention a newspaper, put the title in italics, not quotation marks.

✓ You can assume your reader knows you are available for an interview.

✓ Be correct. Any papers fastened to a cover letter with a clip or staple are *attachments*; papers in the same envelope with the cover letter but not attached to it are *enclosures*.

✓ Monitor usage. Hyphenate *entry-level position*.

✓ Be specific. Cite reasons that you are a strong candidate.

✓ Assure the reader that you will be an asset.

✓ Be correct. Replace *thank-you* with *thank you*. *Thank-you* is an adjective or a noun; *thank you* is a verb.

Cover Letter for Résumé
(Advertised Job, Proficient)

When you respond to an online ad, you may be asked to apply for the job by e-mail, and you may be replying to an employment agency without being given the name of any individual there.

E-Mail to Employment Agency

The Original

To Whom It May Concern:

I have a distinguished record as a sr. grants administrator. Perhaps you will consider me for the position you need to fill. My résumé is attached.

I have worked with nonprofit organizations for a decade and have a good track record with grant application, administration, budgets, and compliance. I am skilled at troubleshooting and could probably work well with your people under pressure.

I am personally concerned with the plight of the homeless and would find it rewarding to make a difference by joining your Helping the Homeless team.

Sincerely,

Drew Grant

The Formula

Beginning: Introduce yourself as a strong candidate for the position.

Middle: Sell yourself, matching your qualifications with those the employer seeks.

End: Close with confidence. If the ad gives a telephone number and does not instruct applicants not to call, say when you will follow up with a telephone call.

E-Mail to Employment Agency

The Makeover

Re: Job ID 96237

I fit the description of the experienced Senior Grants Administrator that Helping the Homeless is looking for. As the attached resume indicates, I will bring to the job:

- An excellent track record with grant applications and administration;
- A firm grasp of the legal issues surrounding grant contracts and of federal, state, and local regulations;
- A solid background in budget management;
- Highly developed interpersonal skills, even under pressure;
- A wide network of contacts developed during my decade in nonprofit organizations.

I hope you agree that these qualifications are an outstanding match with the criteria for the new Senior Grants Administrator for Helping the Homeless. I look forward to hearing from you.

Sincerely,

Drew Grant

Checklist
- ✓ Be specific. If the ad gives a job number, refer to it at the top of your reply. You need not add *To Whom It May Concern*.
- ✓ When you answer an ad placed by a third party hired by the prospective employer to screen candidates, don't address the reader as if she or he is with the organization you hope to join.
- ✓ Monitor usage. Shun indecisive words such as *perhaps* and *probably*, which create doubt in the reader's mind.
- ✓ If the job title is capitalized in the ad, capitalize it, even if capitalization is not correct.

✓ In e-mail, don't put accent marks in *résumé*, because not all e-mail software can handle them; a string of code may appear, making your message difficult to decipher. To further reduce the risk that strings of code may mar your e-mail message, send it in plain text unless you know the recipient's e-mail provider can handle HTML. Similarly, don't put two or more spaces together in an e-mail because in some readers' e-mail, the second space will be converted to code. And for a dash, use two hyphens with a space on either side, to keep them together, looking like a dash: --.

✓ Telegraph ideas. For a vertical list in e-mail, use hyphens for bullet points.

✓ Apply ego check. Instead of describing what you find rewarding, feature the qualifications for this job that the employer will find most important.

✓ Without arrogance, suggest that you are the candidate the employer is seeking.

The Original

Dear Mr. Sandor,

When I phoned your department, I was told to write to you. Due to the fact that I have just graduated from Dirkmann Institute with a BBA, I seek an accountant position at Marley, Chou & Kravitz. My resume is attached and includes my GPA and the courses I took that prepared me for a job as an accountant. I will call you next week about an appointment to discuss job possibilities.

Sincerely,

Geneva Billinsly

Geneva Billinsly

The Formula

Beginning: State what job you seek and refer to your attached résumé.

Middle: Summarize your chief qualifications for an entry-level position.

End: Specify when you will call to discuss the possibility of a job opening.

The Makeover

Dear Mr. Sandor:

I am a recent graduate of the Dirkmann Institute with a degree in accounting. I would like my first job as an accountant to be with Marley, Chou & Kravitz. My résumé is attached.

Because I have had courses in analysis, AP, AR, and accounting and have a 3.0 grade point average, I am qualified for an entry-level position. I can start immediately.

Wednesday morning, June 10, I will call to discuss a possible opening for an accountant with my qualifications.

Sincerely,

Geneva Billinsly

Geneva Billinsly

Checklist

✓ Adjust the tone. Use a colon, not a comma, in the salutation.

✓ No need to tell the reader how you got his name.

✓ Be alert for gobbledygook. Replace *due to the fact that* with *because*.

✓ Ordinarily, use an acronym only after you have given the full name or phrase, for example, *grade point average (GPA)*. But if your reader is sure to know what an acronym means, you don't need to spell it out—for example, someone hiring an accountant should know what AP and AR stand for.

✓ Be empathetic. Say something nice about the company as a place you would like to work.

✓ Be specific. Say when you will call.

✓ Don't assume you will get an appointment. But if you do, write a thank-you note after the interview.

The Original

To the Human Resources Department:

Please find attached my résumé. I am an experienced C-130 flight instructor with security clearance. I have logged 250 hours as a flight instructor/examiner and would like to join Grahamston Aircraft. In brief, I have been responsible for the ground based training of student pilots and many of my suggestions for modifying training courseware, procedures and policies have been adopted. I handle administrative duties well and stay current in all relevant areas.

The next time you have a vacancy for a ground based trainer for C-130 crewmembers, please consider my application.

Sincerely,

Troy Ford

Troy P. Ford

The Formula

Beginning: Tell the reader what job you seek.

Middle: Sell yourself as a top candidate for the position when a vacancy occurs.

End: Refer to your attached résumé, and give the date when you will follow up with a call.

The Makeover

Dear Ms. Cleary:

I would like to join Grahamston Aircraft as a ground-based trainer for C-130 crewmembers.

I have logged 250 hours as a C-130 flight instructor and examiner and have provided ground-based training for student pilots. I contribute to the continued improvement of all aspects of the training process. And I handle administrative duties with the same thoroughness and expertise with which I approach training. At the same time, I stay current in both theory and practice.

For these reasons, I believe I can make a significant contribution at Grahamston. You will find further support for this claim in my attached résumé. I will call you Tuesday afternoon, January 17, to discuss employment possibilities.

Sincerely,

Troy Ford

Troy P. Ford

Checklist

✓ Call to get the name of the person responsible for hiring in your area of expertise.

✓ Weed out such clichés as *please find attached.*

✓ Emphasize key points. The opening is a position of positive emphasis. Sell yourself as a pro.

✓ Avoid redundancy. Mentioning the 250 hours logged makes your experience evident.

✓ In a formal letter, don't use the casual slash, also called a *solidus* or *virgule* (say *instructor and examiner*, not *instructor/examiner*).

✓ Monitor usage. Hyphenate a compound adjective modifying a noun, for example, *ground-based training.* (But don't hyphenate adverb modifiers, which often end in *-ly*, for example, *highly effective training.*)

The Original

Dear Mrs. Schultz:

I am writing to thank you for taking the time to interview me for the position of senior tax manager that you are trying to fill. Working for a "Fortune 500" company such as yours has been my ambition ever since I was in graduate school. At this point in time, my 15 years with O'Hara & Pinkus, CPA, have prepared me for such a move. Once again, many thanks. I hope to have the privilege of working with you.

Respectfully,

Javier Sanchez

Javier Sanchez

The Formula
Beginning: Express thanks for interview.
Middle: Refer to a personal aspect of the interview.
End: Indicate that you want the job.

The Makeover

Dear Mrs. Schultz:

Thank you for the opportunity to discuss the senior tax manager position. You supplied a well-rounded picture of the job's challenges and rewards. I am even more interested in the position because of our conversation.

You will find the article I mentioned on property tax audits enclosed. It makes several good points in areas we discussed.

I look forward to hearing from you and am enthusiastic about the possibility of taking on the responsibilities of senior tax accountant with your prestigious firm.

Sincerely,

Javier Sanchez

Javier Sanchez

Checklist
- ✓ Generally, job applicants do not write a follow-up note of thanks, which makes your writing one a smart move.
- ✓ Get to the point. Instead of stating the obvious (*I am writing*), give your reason for writing.
- ✓ Monitor usage. Don't put *Fortune 500* in quotation marks.
- ✓ Be alert for gobbledygook. Replace *at this point in time* with *now*.
- ✓ Be empathetic. To lump the company you want to work for in with other firms—*a company such as yours*—lacks diplomacy.
- ✓ Say nice things about the company if you can do so sincerely.
- ✓ Sometimes the winning candidate is the one who wants the job most. Say you want the job.
- ✓ Be empathetic. Instead of referring to your current employer, refer to an aspect of the interview that will help the reader remember you as an individual.
- ✓ Don't say *thank you* twice.

The Original

Dear Mr. Cooke:

After a rigorous selection process, I am pleased to offer you the position of Associate Civil Engineer with the Santa Rosa Transit Authority with an annual salary of $66,000.

Your benefits package is comprised of a health care plan that includes dental and vision care; life insurance; and liberal holiday, vacation, and sick leave. The SRTA also contributes to the Public Employees Retirement System.

Upon accepting this offer, you will receive a folder from Human Resources with employment forms to fill in and return.

Please respond in writing to this offer.

Sincerely,

Trisha Prial

Trisha L. Prial
Vice President, Human Resources

TLP:kk

The Formula

Beginning: Offer the job and describe the compensation package.

Middle: Describe benefits or enclose a detailed description of them. Refer to any other relevant aspects of the job offer, for example, an attached contract or letter of agreement.

End: Set a response deadline, and state what form of response is acceptable (phone call, mailed letter, fax, e-mail).

The Makeover

Dear Mr. Cooke:

I am pleased to invite you to join the Santa Rosa Transit Authority (SRTA) as an associate civil engineer with an annual salary of $66,000.

The enclosed employee handbook describes employee benefits in detail. Upon accepting this offer, you will receive a folder from Human Resources with various forms to fill in and return.

Please respond to this offer by postal mail or fax by April 11, 200–.

Sincerely,

Trisha Prial

Trisha L. Prial
Vice President, Human Resources

TLP:kk

Checklist
- ✓ Get to the point. Make the offer. The candidate knows the selection process was rigorous.
- ✓ Be correct. Don't capitalize the job title.
- ✓ Monitor usage. Replace *comprised of* with *comprises* or *is composed of.*
- ✓ To help the prospective new employee make an informed decision, consider enclosing the employee handbook or other documentation that describes employee benefits in detail. These issues can be deal makers or deal breakers.
- ✓ Stick with your organization's policy about what to say in a job offer.
- ✓ Give the deadline for a response.
- ✓ At the bottom of the letter, between the initials of the writer and the typist, either a colon (:) or a slash (/) is acceptable.

The Original

Dear Mr. Kousvitski:

Thank you for offering me a job as a computer programmer, but I cannot accept a salary of $52,000. I feel my qualifications entitle me to $60,000, which was the top salary offered in the ad for the job.

If you can raise the offer now on the table, I would like very much to work for you.

Sincerely,

Martha Yang

Martha Chu Yang

The Formula

Beginning: State that you want to accept the job if the terms are improved.

Middle: State what terms are acceptable, and document your claim to deserving the better terms.

End: Reiterate that you want to work for the organization under mutually acceptable terms; express appreciation for the job offer.

The Makeover

Dear Mr. Kousvitski:

I want to accept your offer of a job as a computer programmer—if we can agree on compensation.

Your offer of $52,000 a year is at the low end of the salary range mentioned in the classified ad that I answered. Yet my qualifications meet or exceed those specified in the ad, which gave $60,000 as the top salary. I believe my services justify a better compensation package. Here is a comparison of the qualifications listed in your ad and those I bring to the job.

What You Require	What I Offer
A. bachelor's degree from an accredited college	A. bachelor's degree from the University of Massachusetts
B. three years of programming experience	B. four years of programming experience
C. proficient communication skills	C. excellent communication skills
D. familiarity with application development	D. expertise in application development
E. experience using PowerBuilder, Norvell 4.11 Client and Server, Windows NT Server 4.0, SQL Server, Windows 2000, Visual Basic, and a scanning management system	E. experience using PowerBuilder, Norvell 4.11 Client and Server, Windows NT Server 4.0, SQL Server, Crystal Reports, Windows 2000, Visual Basic, and Compulink Scanning Management System

If you will improve the compensation package, I will enthusiastically pursue the opportunity to work for Zaytech. In any case, thank you for the offer and for our wide-ranging discussion of what you expect from computer programmers.

Sincerely,

Martha Yang

Martha Chu Yang

Checklist

✓ In the first paragraph, convey your interest in the job offer and state the general reason that you can't accept it under the terms offered. Save the details for the next paragraph.

✓ Instead of referring exclusively to a *salary* or *wage*, refer also to a *compensation package*—leaving the door open for alternative benefit offers such as a guaranteed raise after six months, a company car, fully paid health benefits, flextime, or stock options.

✓ Be empathetic. Stress what you are worth to the employer rather than what you are entitled to.

✓ Avoid redundancy. To prevent ineffective repetition (*offering, offered, offer*), find another way of expressing your idea (e.g., replace *salary offered* with *salary mentioned*).

✓ Supply facts and figures suggesting that you deserve a better offer; this information can help your reader convince other people involved in the hiring decision.

✓ Weed out such clichés as *on the table*.

✓ Close with not only a repetition of your requirement but also a note of appreciation of the prospective employer.

The Original

Mr. Leland K. Swenson
C/O Cabot Investments
1010 Second Avenue
Milwaukee, WI 53200

Dear Mr. Swenson:

Thank you for offering me a job in the secretarial pool at $10 an hour. I really appreciate the opportunity. But as I explained when you interviewed me, I'm a single mom and was concerned that Cabot Investments would charge me more than I can afford to pay to add coverage for my daughter to the health plan. One reason I was looking for a job in the first place was that the one I had didn't provide health coverage for her. Three days later, I was lucky enough to be hired by The Lodge at the Lake at $10 an hour, and coverage for my daughter under their health plan is free to me.

Thank you for the interview. I wish you luck in finding a secretary.

Sincerely,

Carole Tubin

Carole Tubin

The Formula

Beginning: Start with the news that you are declining the job offer. If you care to give a reason, do so succinctly.

Middle: No need for a middle paragraph.

End: You may want to reapply to this employer later, so close in a friendly fashion.

The Makeover

Mr. Leland K. Swenson
Manager, Human Resources
Cabot Investments
1010 Second Avenue
Milwaukee, WI 53200

Dear Mr. Swenson:

With regret, I must decline the job in the secretarial pool because I recently accepted an offer from another employer whose compensation package includes my daughter in the health plan at no cost to me.

Thank you for offering me a position with your prestigious firm. That in itself means a lot to me.

Sincerely,

Carole Tubin

Carole Tubin

Checklist

✓ Be correct. In the address, delete *C/O* and add the addressee's job title.

✓ In the first sentence, state that you are not accepting the job.

✓ Get to the point. If you want to give your reason for turning down a job, confine yourself to the short version.

✓ Be empathetic. Although you may be trying to defuse any hostility that you imagine your reader feels because you didn't accept the job offer, don't say *I wish you luck.* In this context, it might be misread as sarcasm (*Lots of luck!*).

✓ Presumably, you wrote a thank-you letter right after the interview, so find a different positive way to close.

Job Offer
Acceptance

The Original

Dear Andrea:

I am pleased to accept the job as district sales manager and will begin, as requested, on May 17. Please find enclosed the letter of agreement.

I look forward to working with you and increasing district sales.

Sincerely,

Jasper

Jasper Smalley

The Formula

Note: All terms of the job should be in writing—for instance, salary or wages, benefits, hours, vacations, holidays, personal and sick days, perks, amount of travel, office space and clerical support, commissions, opportunities for raises and promotions, and any other aspects of the job that matter to you.

Beginning: Accept the job with pleasure; record the job title, salary, and starting date.

Middle: Refer to the attached contract or letter of agreement that either (a) the employer sent and you signed or (b) you wrote, signed, and require the employer to sign (include a copy for employer and a copy to be returned to you).

End: Say something nice about your new employer; express your confidence that you will be a positive addition to the organization.

The Makeover

Dear Andrea:

I am delighted to accept the job as district sales manager at Western Image Graphics for $90,000 a year, and, as you requested, will begin on May 17.

The letter of agreement, which you sent and I signed, is attached. One small detail that we agreed on was overlooked, so I wrote it in: I will be assigned a parking space next to the building near the south entrance. Please initial this addition (as I did) before you return a copy of the agreement to me.

Meeting you, Kevin, and Mort increased my considerable enthusiasm for working at Western and for giving district sales a healthy boost.

Sincerely,

Jasper

Jasper Smalley

Checklist

✓ Emphasize key points. Specify the salary in the first paragraph (a position of positive emphasis), and mention the name of the organization.

✓ Apply ego check. Does opening both paragraphs with *I* make you look self-centered?

✓ Weed out clichés. Replace *please find enclosed* with *the letter of agreement is enclosed.*

✓ Be correct. If the paperwork is attached, say *attached* not *enclosed.*

✓ Monitor usage. To spare your reader's possible confusion, repeat a preposition before each phrase to which it relates—*look forward **to** working with you and **to** increasing regional sales.*

E-Mail

The Original

In reply to your request for a reference for Samuel Daniels, all I am free to say is that Mr. Daniels was employed by Nationwide Hardware but I cannot provide you with details concerning his departure or his performance while employed here.

Heather Marks

The Formula

Beginning: State your refusal.
Middle: Explain why you are refusing.
End: Supply whatever relevant details organization policy allows.

E-Mail

The Makeover

Dear Ms. Ellsworth:

Our company policy prevents me from granting your request for (a) a reference for Samuel Daniels or (b) details of his employment by, or departure from, our firm.

I can, however, confirm that Mr. Daniels was employed as a sales associate at Nationwide Hardware from January 9, 200–, through September 5, 200–.

Sincerely,

Heather Marks
Manager
Personnel Department

Checklist

✓ For this kind of formal e-mail to someone you don't know, begin with *Dear* and close with *Sincerely.*

✓ Be specific. Put your job title and department under your name at the end.

✓ Explain that your refusal is based on organization policy.

✓ In no way imply that you are withholding a reference because the employee was unsatisfactory; employees have been known to sue former employers for negative references.

✓ If the employee was fired, do not say that unless organization policy is to do so.

✓ Monitor usage. Avoid dangling constructions. *In reply to your request* needs something to modify, for example, *In reply to your request . . . I am free to say only.* The phrase now modifies *I.*

✓ Provide whatever details may be helpful, as long as doing so complies with organization policy.

✓ Telegraph ideas. If you make more than one point in a single sentence, identify the points using a horizontal, lettered list.

✓ Lawyers often influence organization policy on hiring and firing; stick with the policy. And always consult a lawyer if you need legal advice about anything you write.

Rejection of
Promotion Request

The Original

Dear Bob,

I liked seeing that you applied for the vacant Estimator slot. What that means to me is that you want to grow your career at Capstone Industries. But we need an Estimator with qualifications that you currently lack.

Keep reading announcements of openings at Capstone and feel free to follow-up on any that you are fully qualified to take on. Meantime, keep doing well in your currant job.

Regards,

Marv

Marvin A. Lorch
Senior Manager

MAL:zo

The Formula

Beginning: Acknowledge the employee's wish to grow within the company, and mention any valid points the employee made in applying for the promotion.

Middle: Outline ways in which the employee's qualifications do not match the new job.

End: Acknowledge the employee's efforts in his or her current job, and describe any steps to take that will make future promotion likely.

The Makeover

Dear Bob,

Reading your application for the vacant estimator slot, I was glad to see that you are looking for ways to advance at Capstone Industries. As you point out, you have wide experience in paving operations, from design mix to lay-down.

But the estimator will handle not only small jobs but also $12 million jobs, so we need someone who has more experience than you. And we prefer a college graduate.

We are pleased with your performance in your current position. If, however, you want to move up the career ladder, consider completing your college credits in the evening and getting your degree. Capstone has funds available for employees' continuing education, and I will be glad to write a reference.

Cordially,

Marv

Marvin A. Lorch
Senior Manager

MAL:zo

Checklist

✓ Monitor usage. The verb *follow up* does not have a hyphen.

✓ But as an adjective or a noun, follow-up is hyphenated— *Follow up* [verb] on her *follow-up* [adjective] interview, and then confirm your *follow-up* [noun] with me.

✓ Proofread. In the last sentence, *currant* (a fruit) should be *current*. Beware of *homophones*—words that are pronounced the same way but spelled differently, for example, *great/grate, it's/its, overdue/overdo, their/there/they're, to/too/two.*

12

Request
for a Raise

The Original

Dear Mr. Larson,

I hope you won't think I'm being too forward in asking for a raise. I have been the receptionist and also supported the administrative assistants with their overload during my two years at this job, but I never receive a raise. I believe I deserve a $4,000 raise now to keep up with the cost of living and also acknowledge my contribution.

If you think $4000 is too high, please inform me of what you believe a fair raise would be, or if you don't agree that I should have a raise now, please tell me what I can do to earn one as soon as possible.

Respectfully,

Vera Avery

Vera Avery
Receptionist

The Formula

Beginning: State (a) your job title, (b) how long you have been in that position, (c) how long you have been with the organization, (d) what raise you seek, and (e) what your salary or wages would be after the raise.

Middle: Supply convincing evidence that you deserve a raise now; mention any commendations from those inside and outside your organization.

End: Affirm that you like working for the company (if you do) and are good at your job; repeat the amount of the raise you request.

The Makeover

Dear Mr. Larson:

As the receptionist, in addition to my primary duties, I provide ongoing support for administrative assistants by maintaining databases. Yet in my two years at Leadingedge Biotechnology, I have not received a raise. Therefore, I now request a $4,000 raise, which will bring my salary up to $44,000 a year.

You will find attached: (a) a copy of my most recent performance review, on which I received high marks; and (b) a letter in support of this request for a raise from my supervisor, Consuelo Martinez, praising my tact, friendliness, and competence in dealing with people both inside and outside Leadingedge. Moreover, my work with databases is accurate and timely, as the administrative assistants will tell you.

Leadingedge is a good place to work, and I am proud of being a team player here. I have grown in my job and hope you agree that I have earned a $4,000 raise.

Respectfully,

Vera Avery

Vera Avery
Receptionist

Checklist
- ✓ No need to apologize for asking for a raise, but do *ask* for it. (Don't just say you believe you deserve it.)
- ✓ Proofread. Write $4,000 consistently (not $4000, in last paragraph).
- ✓ Note in the first paragraph what your total compensation would be after the raise.

✓ Figure a cost-of-living increase into the requested raise but do not refer to it. If your company does not give cost-of-living increases automatically, they have a tacit or explicit policy against it.

✓ Control verbs. Keep tenses consistent. Instead of "I *have been* the receptionist and also *supported* the administrative assistants . . . , but I never *receive* a raise," write, "I *have been* the receptionist and *have supported* the administrative assistants . . ., but I never *have received* a raise." (Note that *and also* is redundant and is replaced with *and*.) Better still: Use present tense.

✓ You should have collected in writing any commendations from your superiors and have kept a record—with dates, names, and quotations—of compliments about your performance from customers and vendors. Attach copies of these support documents to your request, and refer to them in the middle paragraph.

✓ Why suggest that the raise you are asking for is too high? If you are offered less money than you requested, then you may want to ask management how they arrived at their final offer.

✓ Why suggest that you may not get the raise? If you do not get it, then you can ask for guidance in steps that will lead to a raise.

Recommendation
of a Raise

The Original

Dear Ms. Besharov:

Gayle Dircio joined my department as an entry-level chemist one year ago at a salary of $32,000. She has proved herself conscientious, dedicated, and talented. She started working the third shift and, after six months, requested and was granted a transfer to the second shift at the same salary. That is when I began observing what a good job she does.

This is her first job with a pharmaceutical company, and she has told me she hopes to continue her career here at Delaney Pharmaceuticals. To encourage her to do this and to reward her for her work here, I recommend a raise of $3,000 annually, bringing her salary up to $35,000 annually. She is a team player and already shows leadership skill, even among more seasoned chemists. I hope you will grant her the raise effective June 1, 200–.

Sincerely,

Tyler T. Tyree

Tyler T. Tyree
Senior Chemist

The Formula

Beginning: Specify the amount of the raise and what the employee's salary would be after the raise. Give the name and job title of the employee for whom you seek a raise; note how long the employee has been (a) in that position and (b) with the firm.

Middle: Explain in detail why you are so pleased with the employee's work that you believe a raise is deserved.

End: Repeat the amount of the raise you request and the employee's worthiness of it.

The Makeover

Dear Ms. Besharov:

I recommend an annual raise of $3,000, beginning June 1, 200–, for Gayle Dircio:

◆ Ms. Dircio joined my department as an entry-level chemist one year ago at a salary of $32,000.
◆ The raise would bring her salary up to $35,000 a year.
◆ She worked the third shift for six months and then was granted a transfer to the second shift at the same salary.

Why does she deserve a raise? Because she—

◆ Demonstrates conscientiousness, dedication, and talent;
◆ Shows leadership skills even among more seasoned chemists;
◆ Is a team player;
◆ Wants to continue her career at Delaney.

It is good policy to encourage and reward outstanding employees like Ms. Dircio. I hope you will grant her a $3,000 raise effective June 1. She has earned it.

Sincerely,

Tyler T. Tyree

Tyler T. Tyree
Senior Chemist

Checklist
✓ Emphasize key points. Ask for the raise in the first paragraph.
✓ Revise order. Rearrange the sentences in logical groupings: what you want in the first paragraph; why you want it in the second.
✓ Monitor usage. Repeat a word twice in a single sentence only to add emphasis. In the second paragraph, substitute *a year* for the second *annually*.

14

The Original

Dear Cat,

I've accepted a new position that is a good career move in terms of money and responsibilities. As you know, you told me a promotion and a raise aren't in my future here this year. I really enjoy working at Inclusive Insurance but need to move on. I'll be glad to train my replacement in the remaining time. My last day here will be July 3.

Best wishes,

Don

The Formula

Beginning: State that you are resigning as of a specific date. If you possibly can, give at least two weeks' notice (unless you are in a business where employees are told to leave the same day they resign to discourage them from taking company secrets and accounts with them). Offer to be available for consultations for a period after you leave.

Middle: If you are expected to give notice well in advance and cannot, explain why. Otherwise, omit a middle paragraph.

End: If you want to, briefly explain why you are giving notice. Say something nice about the job you are leaving.

The Makeover

Dear Catherine:

I have enjoyed working at Inclusive Insurance as a file clerk but must now resign. If you wish, I can stay until July 3, 200–. For the following month, I will be available for telephone consultations.

The new job I am moving into represents a promotion in terms of both position and hourly rate—possibilities that you said would not be available this year if I stayed here. While I am happy about the advancement, I will miss my friends at II.

Sincerely,

Don

Donald Siler
File Clerk

Checklist

✓ You may want to tell your supervisor you are leaving before presenting a letter of resignation; leave the letter at the close of the conversation.

✓ State right away that you are giving notice and mention the date of your last day in your current job.

✓ It is responsible to offer to stay for two or more weeks, but do not volunteer to train your replacement. Your supervisor can ask you to do that if a replacement is hired before you leave.

✓ Offer to be available for questions after you leave. Such cooperation may be to your benefit if you ask for a reference later.

✓ Make your salutation and complimentary closing formal; this letter will go in your personnel file (e.g., *Dear Catherine:* not *Dear Cat,* and *Sincerely* not *Best wishes*).

Inside the Organization

15. Notice to Staff of Workshop

16. Persuading Colleagues

17. Invitation to Participate in Company Project

18. Alert to Staff

The Original

To: The Staff
From: Arlene Devlin
Date: [Month —, 200–]
Subject: Dictating Workshop

There's going to be a workshop in Dictation Skills That Save Time presented in-house next month. We don't know why more of you don't record dictation but we want to encourage you to do so. The Department of Labor reports that you can record ideas 6 times faster when you dictate than when you write.

Objections I hear to dictation include "I can't organize my thoughts as well when I talk as when I write," "I forget where I am and what I've said earlier," and "Writing is a comfortable habit but dictating is awkward and unfamiliar." None of these objections stand up. You can make brief notes about what you want to say. You can organize the points you want to make before you begin to dictate so you don't just ramble on and produce a letter or memo that sounds as disorganized as most conversation is. You can use the pause button to stop the tape while you take time out to think about what your objective is in relation to your reader's point of view. You can erase and record over sections that you want to change if you don't like what you've said. When you write something long or complicated, then just dictate the first draft and later edit the hard copy. The more you dictate the easier it gets.

The workshop will take place on Wednesday, June 18, in the twenty-first floor conference room from 9am to noon. There is a limit of 25 participants. Please give my assistant KC (ext. 1234) a list of the people in your department who will attend.

The Formula

Beginning: Announce what training you are offering and why. If it
is free, say so.

Middle: Sell the training to your people and make clear what the
advantages are of gaining this new skill.

End: Cover the logistics.

The Makeover

To: The Staff
From: Arlene Devlin
Date: [Month —, 200–]
Subject: Workshop on Dictation Skills That Save Time

Purpose of Workshop

According to the Department of Labor, dictating enables us to
record ideas six times faster than writing does. To encourage our
managers to make the most of this time management tool, we are
presenting the workshop Dictation Skills That Save Time, which
we urge you to attend at no cost for you.

Common Objections to Dictating

Managers who are reluctant to record dictation often say, when
I dictate,

- I can't organize my thoughts;
- I forget where I am and what I've said earlier;
- I feel more self-conscious than when I write.

Answers to Objections to Dictating

Objections to dictating can be countered with these replies:

- Before you start, make *brief notes* about what you intend to
  say and how you intend to organize your ideas.
- When you write something long or complicated, dictate the
  first draft, and then *edit a hard copy.* Be alert for your own and
  your readers' *unspoken assumptions* and *vague intentions.*

- ◆ Make dictating a *habit*.
- ◆ While dictating, use the *pause button* to stop and think. Erase and rerecord sections you want to change. Pausing gives you extra time to *engage empathy* for your readers and to find a shared perspective on your subject.

Next Steps and Logistics

When: 9 A.M. to noon, Wednesday, June 18, 200–
Where: 21st floor conference room
Limit: 25 people
Sign-up: Please tell K. C. Hollingshead (ext. 1234) you will attend.

Checklist
- ✓ Telegraph ideas. Use the subject line to hook your readers' attention. Outline your main points in headings.
- ✓ Add empty space. Leave a blank line between paragraphs.
- ✓ Emphasize key points. In a list, stress positive versus negative. Use parallel construction (similar sentence structure) for listed items, because it helps you compare and contrast ideas. Highlight appropriate ideas by putting them in italics.
- ✓ Be correct. Write *six* not *6*.
- ✓ Control verbs. Watch subject-verb agreement and replace "None of these objections *stand* up" with "None of these objections *stands* up." *None* (not objections) is the subject of *stands*.
- ✓ Proofread. Replace *9am* with *9 A.M.* (in last paragraph).

Persuading Colleagues

The Original

To: All Employees, Austin

From: Celina Frasee, R.N., Nurse's Office

Date: [Month —, 200—]

About: Flu Shot and Other Inoculations—Second Notice

Very few of you responded to the memo I sent out two weeks ago reminding you that the Nurse's Office at the Austin facility is providing free flu shots to all employees. Flu season last year saw a sharp rise in absenteeism. We do not want that to happen again. Flu is no excuse for absence this year, because you can get a free flu shot now.

The Nurse's Office will give you other inoculations at cost. If you are not currently covered by a tetanus shot, for example, you can get one at the Nurse's Office.

We provide nutrition counseling and have weight loss and exercise plans that are yours for the asking.

You do not need an appointment. Just drop by.

The Formula

Beginning: Tell colleagues what you are suggesting and why.

Middle: Explain how cooperation is in their best interest; mention any additional benefits.

End: Repeat what you want them to do.

The Makeover

To: All Employees, Austin

From: Celina Frasee, R.N., Nurse's Office

Date: [Month —, 200–]

About: Flu Is Not an Excuse for Staying Home This Year!

Who?

All Austin employees are eligible.

What?

This month the nurse's office is giving free flu shots to employees who request them.

Why?

Flu season last hear produced a sharp rise in absenteeism. We don't want that to happen again. Flu is no excuse for absence this year, because you can get a free flu shot now.

Where?

The nurse's office is located at 130 North (on the ground floor just beyond the employee cafeteria).

When?

The nurse's office is open between 7 A.M. and 6 P.M.

How?

Just drop by. You do not need an appointment.

What Else?

The nurse's office will give you a variety of inoculations at cost. If you are not currently covered by a tetanus shot, for example, you can get one at the nurse's office. Or if you are an older employee and want a pneumonia shot, we can provide it.

Other Services?

These services are free and confidential—

◆ Nutritional counseling and programs for weight loss and exercise
◆ Referral to various 12-step programs
◆ Discount coupons for a stop-smoking program
◆ Prenatal counseling and referral

And What's That about Flu Shots?

They're free this month at the nurse's office, and getting one now is a smart move.

Note: Clip art courtesy of Clips Ahoy!, *www.clipsahoy.com*

Checklist

✓ To rally the troops to do something they are resisting (they ignored the first notice), you need to get their attention. How can you *stimulate* them to *respond* by coming in for flu shots? The *stimulus-response strategy* has two steps: (1) decide what *response* you want from your reader; (2) based on what you know about your reader's self-interest, design your letter, memo, fax, or e-mail to *stimulate* the response you want.

(*Author's Note*: I learned about the stimulus-response strategy in 1984 from David Soskin and have been recommending it ever since. Mr. Soskin is president of David Soskin Associates, Inc., a direct marketing, strategic planning, and venture capital firm located in Norwalk, Connecticut.)

✓ Omit the reference to a poor response to the previous announcement of the same offer.
✓ Don't capitalize nurse's office.
✓ Telegraph ideas. Use headings to guide the reader's eye.
✓ Consider using colored, even neon, paper to capture immediate interest.

The Original

To: Executive and Administrative Assistants
From: Jake Sydell, Human Resources Manager
Date: [Month —, 200–]
Subject: *Correspondence Handbook* Revision
Attachment: Volunteer sign-up form

Our *Correspondence Handbook* will be updated and revised. Every letter and memo that goes out of this company must be based on the style, usage, and format contained in the handbook.

We are responding to complaints from many of you that the rules and regulations it requires you to follow are outdated and even impractical today. We have hired Marybeth Haffenmead, a professional writer of books and articles on business correspondence, to revise our handbook. The process will involve your voluntary cooperation and contribution.

Phase I: Ms. Haffenmead will spend several days in our offices in sessions with a dozen of you at a time. She has read the handbook and discussed it with me. We have ideas about the direction to take. But your input is essential. She will be hear to listen to you and record your ideas about what needs changing in the handbook.

Phase II: Ms. Haffenmead will write a draft of the new *Correspondence Handbook*, based in part on your feedback. When we are both satisfied with it, she will spend two days here facilitating workshops to introduce the new handbook to the people who participated in the small discussion groups in Phase I. Your feedback will be recorded. Afterward I and Ms. Haffenmead will discuss it.

Phase III: Ms. Haffenmead will revise the handbook, and after I have approved the final version, it will be printed and distributed throughout the company.

Attached is a sign-up form. If you want to participate in this project, sign the form and have your supervisor sign it. Then drop it in the clearly marked box that is on the reception desk in the human resources department. Your voluntary contribution to this important project will be recorded in your personnel file.

The Formula

Beginning: State the nature and scope of the project. Invite participation.

Middle: Outline the details that are most likely to attract participants. (Attach a more lengthy description if necessary.)

End: Tell employees whom to consult with questions and how to volunteer.

This makeover's headline is too flamboyant for conservative businesses, but do what you can to attract attention.

The Makeover

We Heard You. We're Responding.
Now We Need Your Participation:
Help Us Revise and Update Our
Correspondence Handbook!

To: Executive and Administrative Assistants
From: Jake Sydell, Human Resources Manager
Date: [Month —, 200–]
Subject: *Correspondence Handbook* Revision

Attachment: Volunteer sign-up form

With your voluntary participation, our *Correspondence Handbook* will be updated and revised.

The Problem. Many of you have complained that every letter and memo on company letterhead must be based on the style, usage, and format contained in the handbook, which is seriously outdated.

The Solution. We have hired Marybeth Haffenmead, a professional writer of books and articles on business correspondence, to revise our handbook with your participation.

Phase One. For two days, Ms. Haffenmead will meet with a dozen of you at a time for about an hour so that you can tell her what you like about the handbook, what you don't like—and what changes you advocate.

Phase Two. Based in part on your suggestions, Ms. Haffenmead will write a new *Correspondence Handbook*. Then she will facilitate a half-day workshop here to introduce the new handbook to you and to record your ideas for further improvements.

Phase Three. Ms. Haffenmead, in consultation with me about your feedback, will put a final polish on the handbook. The new edition will be printed and distributed throughout the agency, replacing the current *Correspondence Handbook.*

Your Role. To participate in this project, sign the attached form and have your supervisor sign it. Then drop it in the clearly marked box that is on the reception desk in the human resources department. Your voluntary contribution to this important project will be recorded in your personnel file. And, best of all, you will have a new *Correspondence Handbook* that you have helped to create.

Checklist

✓ Add empty space. Revise and redesign the memo to look inviting.

✓ Telegraph ideas. Use headings. Be empathetic. Feature details of what participants will actually do.

✓ Proofread. Replace *she will be **hear*** with *she will be **here*** (in paragraph on Phase I).

✓ Monitor usage. Replace *I and Ms. Haffenmead* with *Ms. Haffenmead and I.* As a rule, never put yourself first.

✓ Be specific. Include the amount of time volunteers will spend on this project.

✓ Remember that internal public relations come into play here.

18

Alert to Staff

The Original

To: The Staff
From: Dale
Date: [Month —, 200–]
Subject: Requests for illegal information

Just a reminder that if any of you are asked for illegal information, you should not answer, and you should report the incident to me.

I bring up the subject because yesterday when Dawn was at her desk in the reception area, one of the elevator doors opened and an elevator man said, "Miss! Miss! Do you know a bookie?"

Dawn was answering phones and had several people on the line so she didn't look up to see which elevator man it was. She just shook her head, "No."

This morning she mentioned the incident to me.

Bookmakers are illegal in this state. In future, please report any illegalities to me immediately. And my thanks to Dawn for telling me what happened.

The Formula

Beginning: Reveal the subject of the alert.
Middle: Tell the staff what you want them to do.
End: Explain the implications.

The Makeover

To: The Staff
From: Dale
Date: [Month —, 200–]
Subject: How to Handle a Request for Illegal Information

Yesterday, while Dawn was at her desk in the reception area, one of the elevator doors opened, and the elevator man said, "Miss! Miss! Do you know a bookie?" She was answering phones and just shook her head no.

Bookmakers are illegal in this state. The outcome for Beautiful Best Cosmetics—of even such seemingly minor exchanges—can be serious when legal issues are involved. I depend on everyone here to use good judgment, as Dawn did.

You all know this, but now is the time for a reminder: If you are asked for illegal information, refuse to answer—even if you know the answer. And report the incident to me.

Checklist

✓ In an informal in-house memo, starting with a sentence fragment is all right. But a better hook would be to tell the story that prompted you to write the memo. A story or an anecdote tends to make readers more receptive to what they are reading.

✓ Include only details relevant to your intended message; for example, readers don't need to know that Dawn was handling several calls simultaneously.

✓ Control verbs. Watch subject-verb agreement and replace *if any of you **are*** with *if any of you **is*** because *any* is a single subject that takes a single verb (*any is*).

✓ Monitor usage. Don't put *no* in quotation marks because Dawn did not say it.

Clients, Customers, and Others

19

Cover Letter for
Travel Schedule

The Original

Dear Claire,

Your itinerary and airline tickets are enclosed. Your scenes begin shooting the day after you arrive. Here's how it will go.

A studio limo will pick you up early enough to leave ample time for security checks and deliver you to LAX. You'll fly first class to Atlanta where a limo driver will meet you and take you to the Crown Royale, where we've book a suite for you. The kick-off party is in a private dining room at the Plantation Restaurant with a traditional Southern buffet and all the mint juleps you can drink.

A limo will pick you up each morning of your seven-day shoot, take you to the location, pick you up at the location on the last day and take you to the airport. A studio limo will meet you at LAX and take you home.

These details and more are all spelled out on the itinerary. I know you'll be great in the part.

As always,

Gadge Nicholson

GN:bb
Dictated but not read

The Formula
Beginning: Describe the most important enclosures and say you are providing an overview of the schedule.

Middle: Highlight each event in sequence that is covered in the enclosed materials.

End: Sign off cordially.

The Makeover

Dear Claire,

Here are your airline tickets and itinerary. Your scenes begin shooting the day after you arrive. This is what we've arranged for you:

◆ A studio limo will pick you up and deliver you to LAX.
◆ You will fly first class to Atlanta, where a limo driver will meet you. He will be holding a sign with your name on it. He will take you to the Crown Royale Hotel.
◆ The kick-off party is in a private dining room at the Plantation Restaurant with a traditional Southern buffet. A limo will take you there (the company will call your suite to confirm the time).
◆ A limo will pick you up each morning of your seven-day shoot, take you to the location, and return you to the Crown Royale at night.
◆ On the last day, the limo will take you from the location to the airport.
◆ You will fly home first class.
◆ A studio limo will meet you at LAX and take you home.

You will be great in the part (I said so from the start). I look forward to hearing all about the shoot when you get back—I'll call you for lunch.

As ever,

Gadge
(by B. Bertolucci)

Gadge Nicholson

GN:bb

Enclosures: airline tickets; itinerary; list of useful contacts.

Checklist

✓ Telegraph ideas. Use bullet points to list the events on the schedule in chronological order.

✓ Be specific. Include all relevant details. How will Claire get to the restaurant? Is she flying home first class?

✓ Scrutinize what you write for good taste and appropriateness, e.g., many people don't find humor in drinking too much.

✓ Emphasize key points. Confine each paragraph to one main idea. Separate the details of the itinerary from your complimentary last sentence. Reader memory and understanding skyrocket when you assign each major idea its own paragraph. This simple technique increases the odds that your reader will remember what you say.

✓ Be specific. Add an enclosure line and list each item that is enclosed, even items not referenced in the body of the letter—in this case, a list of useful contacts.

Note: If you dictate a letter and ask your secretary to type, proofread, and send it without showing it to you again (perhaps you dictated the letter just before leaving town on business), then ask him or her to make the notation *Dictated but not read* beneath the reference initials (of the person who dictated the letter and the person who typed it). Alternatively, ask him or her to sign your name in the usual place and directly beneath it, in parentheses, to write *by* (followed by his or her initials or signature).

✓ Remember that public relations come into play here. You want to keep the recipient happy.

The Original

Dear Maria,

Kirk is putting the finishing touches on your new telemarketing script—you should have it early next week. Meanwhile, the time has come to consider sending periodic mailings to the list of highly qualified prospects we've put together for you.

Everyone assigned to your account thinks a newsletter would produce the best results for you. One idea for a newsletter to be sent once a quarter is to feature

- testimonials from customers who have switched from using the phone line to connect to the internet to using your DSL service.
- cutting-edge technology stories that help position you as at the forefront in the field.

I'll call you to set up an appointment to discuss the advantageous of direct mail and to present you with several options as to what this might look like.

Sincerely,

Liam

Liam Maxfield
Account Executive

The Formula

Beginning: Sell your firm to the client—mention what you have already done.

Middle: Sell your firm to the client—suggest a new project.

End: Sell your firm to the client—point out that you have more ideas to offer.

The Makeover

Dear Maria,

You will receive your new telemarketing script early next week. The draft I saw was terrific, and Kirk is applying the finishing touches now.

With that project nearing completion, this is a good time to consider sending periodic mailings to the database of your prospective customers. All of us assigned to your account met this morning to discuss your options for a direct-mail campaign. The consensus is that a quarterly newsletter will produce the best results for you.

One possibility is a four-page, quarterly newsletter that is folded in thirds. The addresses and postage go on the middle outside panel, and no envelope is needed, which is a cost-effective format. Each edition would feature

- Testimonials from customers who have switched to your DSL service;
- Cutting-edge technology stories that position you at the forefront of the field.

We have other ideas for you to consider, too. I'll call you Thursday morning about getting together to explore your options for keeping in touch with the list of highly qualified prospects we've put together for you.

Regards,

Liam

Liam Maxfield
Account Executive

Checklist

✓ Be empathetic. In the first paragraph, switch the focus to the reader and emphasize what a great job your firm is doing.

✓ Begin a new paragraph to mention the potential new campaign recommended by the team assigned to the client's account.

✓ Be concise. Replace *newsletter to be sent once a quarter* with *quarterly newsletter*.

✓ Don't mention that client's customers previously used telephone lines for Internet access; the reader knows this.

✓ Adjust the tone. Be personal and replace ***everyone*** *assigned to your account* with ***all of us*** *assigned to your account.*

✓ Be positive. Convey what the proposed newsletter will look like and why it is relatively economical.

✓ In the list, replace the period with a semicolon after the first item.

✓ Proofread. A computer spellchecker doesn't pick up such mistakes as *advantageou*s where *advantages* is meant (in last paragraph).

✓ Be specific. Say when you will call.

✓ Emphasize key points. To aid reader memory, close with a reference to the list of highly qualified prospects that your firm assembled. People tend to remember best whatever is at the beginning and the end—two positions of positive emphasis.

✓ Remember that public relations come into play here. You want to keep the client happy.

Draft 1

The Original

Fax to: Gordon Kearney @ 587-9658
From: Devon Luz
Date: [Month —, 200–]
Subject: Your Shoddy Product

Listen, melon mind, we ordered our name Sandborn in 2' high ice letters for our sales conference but you delivered SandbornE. If you think we're going to pay for the erroneous *e*, you've got ice cubes in your head.

Even spelled correctly, Sandborn is a long name. When it melts all over the carpet, there's a flood. When it melts onto the cord attached to the projector, there's a short—the presentation around which this event was planned was abruptly ended long before it was completed.

You told me the sculpture would last all day. Not enough ice was left after lunch to chill a soda. Try melting your bill down to size if you want to thaw our accounting department.

Draft 2

The Original

Fax to: Gordon Kearny @ 587-9658
From: Devon Luz
Date: [Month —, 200–]
Subject: Required discount

We ordered our company name, Sandborn, in two-foot high ice letters from you for our sales conference, but you delivered SandbornE—a misspelling that caused us embarrassment.

To make matters worse, your ice sculpture melted on the carpet of the hotel conference room and flooded the electrical outlet in the floor. The resulting short circuit interrupted the most important presentation of the day. The hotel's general manager was as angry as we were about this, and you will probably hear from her, too.

You told me the ice sculpture would last all day. This was a considerable misrepresentation of your product. Your bill was the only aspect of the original agreement between us that was as agreed. Please send your drastically reduced invoice directly to me within five days.

Author's Note: A similar version of this letter has appeared at my Web site (*www.writeassets.com*) and in handouts created for my corporate writing workshops.

The Formula
Beginning: Announce what is wrong.
Middle: Provide details.
End: Declare what you expect reader to do next, and give deadline
    if appropriate.

Fax to: Gordon Kearny @ 587-9658
From: Devon Luz
Date: [Month —, 200–]
Subject: Meltdown of Ice Sculpture

Dear Mr. Kearney:

The ice sculpture of our company name, Sandborn, which you supplied on November 5 for our sales conference, (1) misspelled Sandborn and (2) melted quickly instead of slowly. I'm sure this is not what you intended, but you are the one we are asking to adjust the invoice to reflect the fiasco.

Misspelling and Meltdown

1. Sandborn has no final *e,* but your ice sculpture did.
—You bill by the letter.
—Do not bill us for the erroneous *e.*

2. You assured me that the ice sculpture would last all day, but it melted onto the meeting room's floor and was forming a puddle there when we returned from lunch. I don't doubt that your assurances to me were made in good faith, but the fact remains that the sculpture you were contracted to provide is not what we received, and the consequences for us were entirely negative.

— The ice water soaked the carpet. We have instructed the hotel manager to bill you directly for the cost of repairing the damage.

— The water from the melting ice pooled around the projector's plug, which was inserted into an electrical outlet on the floor, and the projector went dark during our most important presentation.

Next Steps

Due to the breach of contract described above, we expect you to reduce the invoice by 90 percent. Please send the corrected bill directly to me rather than to our accounting department.

Sincerely,

Devon Luz

Devon Luz
Corporate Meeting Planner

DL:ac

Checklist

✓ Adjust the tone. It is therapeutic to vent anger in a letter, memo, fax, or e-mail, but sending an angry communication is folly.

Note: Whenever you can, allow your reader to save face, regardless of the righteousness of your position. Offer readers alternatives. Grant them the benefit of the doubt. Make room for them to compromise or to come around to your side. If you insist that you are right, then, by implication, they are wrong, and they are apt to become defensive. People who feel defensive are too busy trying to repair their egos to cooperate.

✓ Telegraph ideas. Emphasize your strongest points by placing them in the subject line, in headings, and in lists. Make *Next Steps* a heading when you want the reader to do something.

✓ Be specific. Tell readers exactly what you want done.

✓ Don't give a deadline unless you will benefit from a timely response; in this case, you are not going to pay the bill until you receive a discount, so you have no reason to press for a resolution. (If the vendor were refusing to give you a discount and planned to turn the invoice over to a collection agency, then you would need to arrive at a resolution immediately.)

22

Complaint
about Bank Errors

The Original

Fax to: Leo Mills @ 987-4546
From: Chantrell Gingerich
Date: [Month —, 200–]
Subject: Bank Error

You returned the rent check (#1653) for our boutique, saying we had insufficient funds to cover it. Actually, we did have enough in the account to cover the rent. I don't know why your people thought we didn't. An oversight?

Ten days ago we deposited a check for $14,000, drawn on another of your branches. According to your small-business department, that amount was never credited to our account until I called. The girl I spoke with said she was crediting our account with the check retroactively. We then told our landlord to redeposit our rent check. Will you please honor it this time?

The Formula

Beginning: Write to the bank manager; state the problem, and summarize the bank's errors.

Middle: Give the history of the errors.

End: Demand immediate correction of the errors. Instruct the manager to write letters of apology and explanation to your creditors and to you, to shield your credit rating from negative consequences of the bank's error—and to telephone you confirming that everything required has been done. Set a deadline. Follow up.

Fax to: Leo Mills @ 987-4546
From: Chantrell Gingerich
Date: [Month —, 200–]
Subject: Check #1653 bounced by bank's error; account, #72864319

Our landlord notified me that your bank refused to honor the rent check for our boutique—Rain or Shine Umbrellas & Parasols—claiming that we had insufficient funds to cover it. We had, in fact, more than enough in our firm's account to cover the check.

Chain of Events:
1. Ten days ago, we deposited a check by mail for $14,000.
2. We never received a deposit confirmation.
3. I called the bank this morning and spoke to Betsy Klein in your small-business services department. She said that the $14,000 was received but was not, through a bank error, credited to our account.
4. She credited the $14,000 retroactively.
5. We asked our landlord to redeposit our rent check.

Attachments. A copy of our landlord's letter to us and a copy of our deposit slip comprise the next two pages of this fax.

Our Requirements. We expect you to (a) honor the check when the bank receives it again; (b) write letters this week to us and to our landlord explaining—and apologizing for—the bank's error; (c) ensure that our credit rating is not affected.

Next Step. In addition, please call me at 777-6543 to assure me that you got this fax and will prevent a similar error from occurring in the future.

Chantrell Gingerich

Checklist

✓ Put the essential references in the subject line at the top—in this case the problem and the relevant check and account numbers.

✓ Be specific. Give an orderly description of the problem, providing relevant details. Explain what you expect the reader to do, and include a deadline.

✓ Shun sexism. *Girl* is offensive to many women.

✓ Adjust the tone. In business-to-business complaints, be as cordial as possible. But if your credit record is threatened, as in this case, you need not only to get the situation corrected but also to alert the bank manager that you expect no such errors to happen again.

✓ Be specific. Get the name of anyone you speak to at the bank about the error and include it in your complaint.

✓ A question draws in the reader to what you are saying, but why end *both* paragraphs with a question?

✓ Attach any supporting documents.

Cover Letter for
Marketing Materials

23

The Original

Dear Mr. Reid:

Thank you for your interest in holding your annual conference at Palm Plaza Hotel. We meet your specifications and can supply everything you need. Plus your people will have the pleasure of visiting a very popular resort destination.

Another advantage is that because our property is so extensive, your attendees will not be tempted to leave scheduled meetings in order to shop and sightsee off property but will confine those activities to the times you have set aside for them.

Please find enclosed a folder containing everything you need to plan a successful meeting.

Because your conference is planned for our busiest season, I urge you to reserve the sleeping and meeting rooms you need right away. I look forward to hearing from you.

Warm regards,

Marissa

Marissa Thayer
Director of Sales

MT:nw

The Formula

Beginning: Establish that the enclosed material was requested, if it was, or explain why it is in the reader's interest to look at it.

Middle: Sell your service or product.

End: State what the next steps are to close a deal.

The Makeover

Dear Mr. Reid:

Here is the information you requested about Palm Plaza Hotel. Palm Plaza is the perfect setting for your annual conference.

The Place to Be. The fact that Palm Plaza is such a popular resort destination will help you attract attendees. At the same time, our property is so extensive and beautifully landscaped that attendees are not apt to leave scheduled meetings to shop and sightsee; they are more likely to confine those activities to the times you have set aside for them. Many meeting planners tell me this is key to a successful conference.

Everything You Need. The enclosed folder contains everything required to plan a great meeting at Palm Plaza.

- **Catering:** menus for meals, breaks, and your final banquet.
- **Meetings:** floor plans for our meeting and break-out rooms giving their dimensions and the numbers of people each will hold, depending on the seating arrangement; and a price list for audiovisual equipment.
- **Business Services:** a list of services that include Internet access for laptop computers in guest rooms and a business center with photocopiers, computers, and fax machines.
- **Location:** brochures that describe the Palm Plaza's amenities, such as the pool, fitness facility, tennis courts, and golf course; a sightseeing guide created especially for our guests; and maps showing how accessible we are by plane and car.

Your conference is planned for our busiest season, so I urge you to reserve your guest and meeting rooms as soon as possible. I look forward to hearing from you.

Cordially,

Marissa

Marissa Thayer
Director of Sales

MT:nw

Checklist

✓ Telegraph ideas. Putting a text box containing key ideas above the salutation may increase reader response.

✓ Be empathetic. In the first paragraph, establish for the primary reader (or the primary reader's secretary) that the enclosed material was requested.

✓ In the second paragraph, make your strongest selling point.

✓ In subsequent paragraphs, list the enclosed materials in detail.

✓ Don't use *plus* as a synonym for *and* unless you know it won't annoy your readers.

✓ Emphasize key points. Appealing to readers' self-interest in the first two levels of information (title or subject line, text box, headings, lists, words in italics and boldface, one-line paragraphs, indented sentences, and the first and last sentence) is the surest way to draw them into the third level (block text). Redesign the letter to incorporate all three levels.

✓ Remember that public relations come into play here. You want the prospect to choose your property over all others he considers.

The Original

Fax to: [Name of Vendor]
Fax: [Vendor's fax number]
From: Angela LoBianco
Date: [Month —, 200–]
Subject: Catering

Dear Caterer:

Eucalyptus Publishing has decided to hire a vendor on a year's contract to bring a catering cart into our offices three times a day. We want coffee/tea, sodas, bagels, sweet rolls, etc. in the morning. Sodas, mineral waters, sandwiches, salads, etc., at lunch. And healthy snacks like fruit juices and fruit plus desserts in mid-afternoon. The vendor will have exclusive catering rights here and will circulate the carts through all three floors of our offices. Employees will pay the vendor directly for whatever food they buy.

   Please submit your proposal for this contract to me by postal mail along with sample menus and prices as well as references from satisfied clients, which I will pass along to our Editor in Chief.

Sincerely,

Angela LoBianco

The Formula

Beginning: Summarize what you want proposal to cover.

Middle: Supply comprehensive details of what you require.

End: Give deadline and contact information; promise to let vendor
   know when you have made a decision.

Fax to: [Name of Vendor] @ [Vendor's Fax number]
Attn: [Name of person responsible for responding to RFP]
From: Angela LoBianco, Assistant to the Managing Editor
Date: [Month —, 200–]
Subject: Request for Proposal (RFP)

Dear [Name of person responsible for responding to RFP]:

We request a proposal for a year's contract, to begin September 15, 200–, for a catering cart to circulate through our three floors of offices three times a day, Monday through Friday—serving 32 employees.

Terms. The vendor who wins the contract will have exclusive catering rights here for a year. At the end of the year, we will evaluate the experience and decide if we want to continue. Our employees will pay the vendor directly for whatever food they buy.

Schedule and Menus

1. **8:30 A.M.** Breakfast items including brewed coffee (caffeinated and decaffeinated); hot water with teabags (herbal and caffeinated); chilled juices, sodas, and mineral waters; baked goods such as bagels, sweet rolls, nonfat muffins; and assorted yogurts.

2. **11:30 A.M.** Selection of vegetarian and nonvegetarian sandwiches and salads, with at least two low-fat choices each day; individual bags of a variety of chips; chilled juices, sodas, and mineral waters; assorted yogurts; fresh fruit; and cookies.

3. **2:30 P.M.** Snacks including fresh fruit; cheese and crackers; baked goods such as brownies, cookies, and nonfat muffins; assorted yogurts; chilled juices, sodas, and mineral waters; brewed coffee (caffeinated and decaffeinated); and hot water for tea (herbal and caffeinated).

What to Include in Your Proposal

◆ Sample menus, with prices, for the daily catering listed above

◆ Your brochure, publicity packet, or other marketing materials

◆ References from satisfied customers, with the names of people we may contact to discuss their experiences with your firm

Deadline. We need the proposal by Friday, April 7.

Process. If you are interested in this RFP, please submit your proposal to me by postal mail at the address at the top of this fax. Our management will review all proposals. I will let you know their decision by May first. Meanwhile, feel free to contact me with questions: my telephone is 983-3764; my fax is 983-4298; and my e-mail address is Angela_LoB@~~~~~.com.

Sincerely,

Angela LoBianco

Checklist

✓ Be specific. Include your job title.

✓ Make the subject *Request for Proposal (RFP)*.

✓ Write directly to the person responsible for responding to RFPs.

✓ Monitor usage. Replace *coffee/tea* with *coffee and tea*. A slash mark is too casual a way to say *and*.

✓ Open with a summary of what you are requesting.

✓ Telegraph ideas. Label paragraphs with headings that help the reader spot your main points. Use numbered and bulleted lists.

✓ Be specific. Cover everything that matters to you: Do not assume vendor knows. State how many employees will be served and when the contract will begin. Give deadlines for the proposal's submission and for your final decision. Give information on how to contact you.

The Original

Fax to: Ridley Gross @ 235-2356
From: Henry Lugo
Date: [Month —, 200–]
Subject: Documentation

Please furnish without further delay and to our complete satisfaction documentation for your recently submitted invoice (#3167) including a list of any and all purchases by our personnel from your company during the month in question with dates and complete photocopies of the signatures of the pertinent individuals in our company who signed any such receipts for the items you are charging us for on the above referenced invoice.

The Formula

Beginning: List what you want.

Middle: If necessary, sketch the background of your request.

End: If you want a timely response, say so, but if speed is more important to the reader than to you, don't set a deadline.

The Makeover

Fax to: Ridley Gross at 235-2356
From: Henry Lugo
Date: [Month —, 200–]
Subject: Documentation

To ensure payment of your invoice #3167, please send me: (1) an itemized list of all purchases and (2) photocopies of dated, signed receipts.

Checklist
- ✓ On first line, state your reason for writing.
- ✓ Be concise. Replace *any and all purchases* with *all purchases.*
- ✓ Be alert for such gobbledygook as *without further delay, to our complete satisfaction,* and *above-referenced invoice.*
- ✓ Break up the too-long sentence into two or more shorter sentences.

Rejection
of Vendor

E-Mail

The Original

Lynette, I hope you won't take this in the wrong way because I mean it to be helpful. But it might be a good idea to research your prospective clients before you contact them. Our founders have had a lot of coverage that you can find on the internet, and if you read their bios you'd know they're not only vegetarians, they're outspoken advocates of animal rights. That's the reason why we just aren't a qualified prospect for the feathers and shells you want to sell us. We only use manmade materials.

The Formula

Beginning: Build a bridge of sympathy to the vendor.

Middle: Bury the rejection in the middle, justifying it while allowing the vendor to save face.

End: Emphasize any positive aspects of the situation.

E-Mail

The Makeover

Dear Lynette:

In the photographs you submitted, your feathers and shells look attractive.

But the founders of Baubles and Beads are both vegetarians and animal rights activists. The company practices what they preach, so we never use feathers or shells.

If, however, you decide to market synthetic materials that meet our criteria, we will be happy to consider using them.

Sincerely,
Luisa Alfassi

Checklist
- ✓ Be empathetic. Open with a sentence that prepares the reader for bad news.
- ✓ Adjust the tone. It is all too easy when writing e-mail to slip into inappropriate familiarity and to give unsolicited advice and sound unprofessional.
- ✓ Monitor usage. *Not only* should be followed by *but also*. Replace *reason why* with *reason* because *reason why* is a tautology.
- ✓ Provide adequate detail but don't overdo it.
- ✓ If you can leave open any doors to the future, so much the better.
- ✓ Shun sexism. Replace *manmade* with *synthetic*.

Note: If *man* were an inclusive term that refers also to women, we wouldn't pause over this sentence: "Men no longer drink and smoke when they are pregnant."

- ✓ Remember that public relations come into play here. You don't want the vendor saying unpleasant things about your company.

The Original

Dear Jeremy:

I won't bore you with the details but the bottom line is someone in inventory control (who was terminated as a result) wasn't doing his job and we've run out of stock on several important items unexpectedly. Needless to say we're in "crisis mode" and we depend on you to fill the attached order at once. Please call if there's a problem with this.

Sincerely,

Dustin Bodack

Dustin Bodack
Vice President

DB/se
CC: Rosemary Leftwich, Mimi Vega, Tom Crane, Pat Stein, Attachment (1)

The Formula

Beginning: Say what you need, why you need it, and when you need it.

Middle: Express gratitude in proportion to the special treatment you hope to receive.

End: Say when you will follow up.

The Makeover

Dear Jeremy:

Please rush the attached order through as fast as you can. We have run out of stock unexpectedly and need new supplies at once. Will you help us out?

To be sure you got this order and to check on its status—as well as to thank you personally for whatever you can do to speed up the shipment—I'll call you Thursday morning.

Sincerely,

Dustin Bodack

Dustin Bodack
Vice President

DB/se
Attachment (1)
C: Tom Crane, Rosemary Leftwich, Pat Stein, Mimi Vega
By overnight delivery

Checklist

✓ Get to the point: Don't explain first, explain second.
✓ Avoid telling outsiders about problems within your organization.
✓ Monitor usage. *CC:* means *carbon copy*; *C:* for *copy* is more accurate. The copy line follows the attachment or enclosure line.
✓ Revise order. List names on the copy line in alphabetical order or by seniority.
✓ Be correct. In some cases, it is better to start a new sentence than to add a comma and run on. However, if the sentences here are not shortened, commas should be added as follows: . . . *the details,* . . . *his job,* . . . *Needless to say,* . . . *crisis mode,* . . .
✓ Monitor usage. Don't put *crisis mode* in quotation marks. Quotation marks should never be used for emphasis.

TWO
Provide Information

Inside the Organization:
Announcements and Notices

Clients, Customers,
and Others:
Announcements and Notices

Short Reports

Inside the Organization: Announcements and Notices

28. Policy Change

29. Vesting in Employee Stock Ownership Plan (ESOP)

30. Employer-Assisted Housing (EAH) Program

31. Promotion

32. Retirement

33. Employee Mediation Program

34. Acceptance of Employee Suggestion

35. Change in Procedures

36. Sales Figures

37. Instructions Update

Policy Change

The Original

To: All Employees
From: Elizabeth Mazeaud, President
Date: [Month —, 200–]
About: Thanksgiving
Att: Turkey voucher

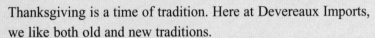

Thanksgiving is a time of tradition. Here at Devereaux Imports, we like both old and new traditions.

As always, you will receive a turkey the day before Thanksgiving (your turkey voucher is attached to this memo). But that's not all! We are changing our policy about being open the day after Thanksgiving. We will close on Friday, too, so you can enjoy a four day holiday.

Note: Clip art courtesy of Clips Ahoy!, *www.clipsahoy.com*

The Formula

Beginning: Announce what the policy change is and when it takes effect.

Middle: Explain how employees will be affected.

End: Point out positive aspects of the change, from the employees' point of view.

The Makeover

To: All Employees

From: Elizabeth Mazeaud, President

Date: [Month —, 200–]

Att: Turkey voucher

About: Thanksgiving

Thanksgiving is a time of tradition. At Devereaux, we like to honor established traditions and to start new ones.

The Devereaux tradition of giving every employee a turkey the day before Thanksgiving will continue, with our good wishes for a happy holiday. (Employees who want to donate their turkey to the Downtown Coalition's homeless shelter should note that choice on their turkey voucher and give it to Greg McCabe in personnel.)

But that's not all. To show our appreciation for all that our employees contribute to our success, Devereaux's new policy, beginning this year, is to *close both Thursday and Friday*. Enjoy your four-day weekend!

Note: Clip art courtesy of Clips Ahoy!, *www.clipsahoy.com*

Checklist

✓ In this case, where the policy change will be greeted with enthusiasm, revealing it at the end of the memo is in the tradition of saving the best for last. But normally, a policy change should be announced in the first paragraph.

✓ Telegraph ideas. Move the subject line to the bottom of the headings so it is easy to spot.

✓ Be concise. Replace *here at Devereaux Imports* with *at Devereaux*.

✓ Monitor usage. Hyphenate *four-day holiday*.

✓ Be empathetic. If you have a number of vegetarian employees, find non-turkey clip art that everyone will like.

✓ After setting up a theme such as tradition in the first paragraph, carry it through in later paragraphs.

Form Letter

The Original

Dear [Employee's name]:

Now that you have worked for Wendell Cranston Vineyards for two years, you are fully vested and have access to your funds in our Employee Stock Ownership Plan (ESOP), which you chose to participate in when you were offered that opportunity after a year of service.

WCV is a private closely held company. That means you cannot sell the shares except to the company. And by federal law, you cannot sell them except under certain circumstances. You need do nothing now unless one of these circumstances applies to you:

◆ When your employment at WCV ends—or due to death, disability, or retirement the funds are dispersed.

◆ If, by the time you are 55 years old, you have participated in the ESOP for at least ten years, you may choose to diversify up to 25 percent of your ESOP.

◆ At age 60, you have a one-time chance to diversify up to 50 percent of your account.

Through the ESOP, you own stock in WCV, which makes you one of the owners of the vineyard. The plan is an enhancement of our employee benefit plan. As a part owner, Mr. Cranston hopes that ESOP participants feel a heightened sense of investment and pride in, and responsibility toward, the vineyard.

Sincerely,

Edgar G. MacLean
Executive Assistant to Mr. Cranston

The Formula

Note: As with anything you write that may have legal implications, consider asking the appropriate lawyer to check written materials you plan to give employees.

Beginning: Announce that the employee is fully vested in the ESOP.

Middle: Explain what that means in practical terms.

End: Support the employee's pride in participating.

Form Letter

The Makeover

Dear [Employee's name]:

You have worked for Wendell Cranston Vineyards (WCV) for two years and are fully vested. You now have access to your funds in our Employee Stock Ownership Plan (ESOP), which you chose to participate in when you were offered that opportunity after a year of service.

WCV is a private closely held company. That means you can sell your ESOP shares only to the company. And by federal law, you can sell them only under certain circumstances. You need do nothing now unless one of these circumstances applies to you. Funds are dispersed when

- ◆ Your employment at WCV ends—due to your resignation, death, disability, or retirement;
- ◆ You are age 55, have participated in the ESOP for at least ten years, and choose to diversify up to 25 percent of your account;
- ◆ You are age 60 and opt for a one-time chance to diversify up to 50 percent of your account.

The ESOP is an enhancement of our employee benefit plan. By owning stock through the ESOP, you are a part owner of the vineyard. Mr. Cranston hopes that as a part owner, you feel a heightened sense of investment in, and responsibility toward, WCV. Moreover, you share in the vineyard's success and can take personal pride in its growing reputation as a producer of fine wine.

Sincerely,

Edgar G. MacLean
Executive Assistant to Mr. Cranston

Checklist

✓ Shorten the first sentence.

✓ Monitor usage. When you use a contraction, which includes a subject and a verb—*you're*—and then add another verb—*have access*—for which *you* is also the subject but to which *are* does not belong, then repeat *you*: **you** are fully vested and **you** have access (first sentence, opening paragraph).

✓ Be positive. Instead of concentrating on when employees cannot sell shares, tell them when they can sell shares.

✓ Use parallel construction for the list of circumstances under which employees can sell shares; that is, use similar sentence structure to compare or contrast similar ideas.

✓ Monitor usage. Look out for misplaced modifiers. The sentence says that Mr. Cranston is a part owner (*as a part owner, Mr. Cranston*) but, in fact, he holds the most shares. Revise to read: *Mr. Cranston hopes that as a part owner, you . . . .* Now *part owner* modifies *you*, as it should.

The Original

To: All Employees
From: Verna Ericson, Director of Human Resources
Date: [Month —, 200–]
Subject: Employer-Assisted Housing Program

In keeping with a growing national trend, Gulf States Health Plan (GSHP) now offers an employer-assisted housing (EAH) program. Our EAH package features a $5,000 loan for the purchase of a home. The loan will be forgiven if the employee stays with us for five years. We will also help negotiate the lowest possible mortgage with a local bank.

This win-win program enables employees to fulfill the dream of owning their own home and, at the same time, encourages them to stay with GSHP. EAH packets are available in the human resources office (room 1411).

The Formula

Beginning: Announce the new plan.

Middle: Give details that help employees decide if they are interested.

End: Provide instructions on how to get more information.

The Makeover

To: All Employees
From: Verna Ericson, Director of Human Resources
Date: [Month —, 200–]
Subject: Employer-Assisted Housing Program

In keeping with a growing national trend, Gulf States Health Plan (GSHP) now offers an employer-assisted housing (EAH) program:

◆ Our EAH package features a *$5,000 loan* for the purchase of a home.

◆ The *loan is forgiven* if the employee *stays with us* for five years.

◆ We will also help negotiate the *lowest possible mortgage* with a local bank.

This win-win program enables employees to fulfill the dream of owning their own home and, at the same time, encourages them to stay with GSHP.

EAH packets are available in the human resources office (room 1411).

Checklist

✓ Telegraph ideas. This memo is an example of an Original that does not need to be rewritten but does need to be redesigned to make its main points easy to spot.

✓ Remember that internal public relations come into play here. One reason your company offers the loans is to keep employees from quitting.

E-Mail Sent to Distribution List

The Original

To: Public Relations Staff
From: Al Nantz
Subject: Promotion

Resheba Jones has been promoted to the position of senior trade show manager from her current position as a manager. She will run our in-house trade show department and report directly to me. Trade show department managers and associates will report to Resheba. All national and international shows will be planned and managed by her. She will also attend the regional shows, overseeing on-site set-ups and post-show teardowns of booths of 4,000 square feet and larger. At the same time that she is supervising a trade show booth, she will maintain long-distance management of other shows. Internally, she will manage special events and incentive programs.

Let's make a point of congratulating Resheba on this significant recognition of her hard work and abilities.

The Formula
Beginning: Tell who is being promoted to what position as of what date.
Middle: Explain how the promotion affects the chain of command, and summarize the main responsibilities of the position.
End: Congratulate the person being promoted.

The Makeover

To: Public Relations Staff
From: Al Nantz
Subject: Promotion of Resheba Jones to Senior Trade Show
Manager

On September 6, Resheba Jones will be promoted from manager to senior trade show manager. She will report directly to me. Trade show department managers and associates will report to her.

Resheba will run our in-house trade show department as well as plan and manage all national and international shows. For regional shows, she will be on site—overseeing our booths from setup to teardown. And from the regional shows, she will also maintain long-distance control of other shows. Internally, she will manage special events and incentive programs.

Congratulations, Resheba, on this recognition of your hard work and your outstanding abilities!

Checklist

✓ Be specific. In the subject line, indicate who is being promoted and to what position.

✓ Give the date when the promotion becomes effective.

✓ Avoid redundancy. Replace *the position of senior trade show manger* with *senior trade show manager*.

✓ Explain in the first paragraph to whom Resheba will report and who will report to her.

✓ Control verbs. Prefer active to passive verbs and replace *all . . . shows will be planned and managed by her* with *She will plan and manage all . . . shows*.

✓ Repeat the modifier *her* so readers who skim won't misread the last sentence as *her hard work and (hard) abilities*.

✓ Be concise. Stick to details readers need.

The Original

Dear Students, Teachers, and Administrative Staff:

Rocco Tarantino will retire at the end of this semester!

Rocco has been the janitor at Middletown Elementary School for 40 years. He's always done a very good job and related very well to everyone else in our school community!

We will miss him but hope he enjoys his retirement!

Sincerely,

Rosalinde Ferguson

Rosalinde Ferguson
Principal

RF/ce

The Formula

Beginning: Announce who is retiring, from what position, and when.

Middle: Say nice things about the retiring employee, both as a person and in a professional capacity.

End: Wish the employee a happy retirement.

The Makeover

Dear Students, Teachers, and Administrative Staff:

Rocco Tarantino, the janitor at Middletown Elementary School for forty years, will retire at the end of the school year. It's hard to imagine our school without Rocco. He has been keeping us clean, cheering us up, and cheering us on for as long as we can remember.

If anyone ever deserved to take it easy, have a second cup of coffee while he reads the sports page, play with his grandchildren, and spend time on the road with his wife and dog in his new, state-of-the-art recreational vehicle, that person is Rocco.

Enjoy your retirement, Rocco. Try not to miss us as much as we'll miss you!

Sincerely,

Rosalinde Ferguson

Rosalinde Ferguson
Principal

RF/ce

Checklist
- ✓ Be specific: Include who, what, and when in the first sentence.
- ✓ Monitor usage. *He's* can be read either as *he is* or *he has*; better to say *he has* in this case.
- ✓ Be correct. Spell *forty*.
- ✓ Monitor usage. Minimize or eliminate the use of *very*, because it tends to have the opposite effect of that intended—it weakens a sentence.
- ✓ An excess of exclamation marks is no substitute for genuine warmth.
- ✓ Be empathetic. Talk to the employee before you write the announcement and, if he agrees, say a bit about what he looks forward to doing as a retiree.

The Original

To: All Employees
From: Elisa Sandoval
Date: [Month —, 200–]
Subject: New Mediation Program

At Fredrick Semiconductors, we need your full attention on your jobs, which don't leave any room for error. But conflicts sometimes occur, and the diversity of our corporate culture (one of the reasons that we enjoy working here) may occasionally give rise to clashes. Interpersonal conflicts are very distracting and keep those involved from doing their best work. For these and other reasons, we are instituting an employee mediation program. The gatekeeper for the program is Ulf Seaberg.

If you have a conflict—with a peer, a subordinate, or a superior—that you are unable to solve, you can go to Ulf to request mediation. Ulf will then contact anyone else involved in the dispute. If the other parties will agree to mediation, Ulf will contact YLN Mediation Services, the firm we have contracted with, and they will arrange a date for mediation.

Compared to the resolution achieved in the courts or through arbitration, mediation gives participants less stress and more control—along with the leeway to explore the options without worrying about the consequences. And the odds that mediation will succeed are better than nine to one.

Contact Ulf Seaberg if you want a confidential discussion about the possibility of participating in mediation or drop by his office for literature explaining mediation in greater depth.

The Formula

Beginning: Announce the program.

Middle: Explain how it works and what the benefits are for participants.

End: Invite participation.

The Makeover

To:	All Employees	**Date:**	[Month —, 200–]
From:	Elisa Sandoval	**Subject:**	New Mediation Program

At Fredrick Semiconductors, your attention should always be on your jobs, which don't leave room for error. But conflicts occur, and the diversity of our corporate culture (one reason we enjoy working here) may occasionally give rise to clashes. Interpersonal conflicts are distracting and keep those involved from doing their best work. For these and other reasons, we are instituting an employee mediation program.

The gatekeeper for the mediation program is Ulf Seaberg.

How Mediation Works

First Steps. If you have a conflict—with a peer, a subordinate, or a superior—that you are unable to solve, you can go to Ulf to request mediation. Ulf will contact anyone else involved in the dispute. If the other parties agree to mediation, Ulf will contact YLN Mediation Services, the firm we have contracted with, and they will arrange a date for mediation.

The Mediation. The parties to the dispute may bring friends, colleagues, or relatives for moral support during the mediation. Each disputant gives her or his version. The mediator listens impartially and helps disputants communicate with each other. In this way, participants can not only arrive at a win-win solution but also gain skills for resolving future conflicts. What is said during mediation is confidential.

Advantages of Mediation

Compared with resolution achieved in the courts or through arbitration, mediation gives participants less stress and more control—along with leeway to explore options without worrying about consequences. *And the odds that mediation will succeed are better than nine to one.*

How to Explore Mediation

Contact Ulf Seaberg (extension 153) to schedule a confidential discussion about the possibility of participating in mediation—or drop by his office (390 South) for mediation literature.

Checklist

✓ This memo does not need much revision of text but does need a quick fix—redesign it so readers can skim and review the information easily.

✓ Telegraph ideas. Group them under headings, which aid reader memory.

✓ Be concise. See how many extraneous words you can delete.

✓ Emphasize key points. For those who read only one-line paragraphs, make the sentence about Ulf being the gatekeeper a one-sentence paragraph.

✓ Monitor usage. Use *compared to* when you want to liken things and people; use *compared with* to weigh similarities and differences.

✓ Be correct. In the last sentence, insert a comma or dash between *mediation* and *or.*

✓ Be specific. Tell readers how to contact Ulf. And explain the meditation process.

✓ Remember that internal public relations come into play here. You need employee support if the program is to succeed.

34

Acceptance of Employee Suggestion

The Original

To: Aaron Kidder
From: Erin Nylund
Date: [Month —, 200–]
Subject: Your suggestion

Congratulations! The suggestion you put in the employee suggestion box that we add a salad bar to the employee cafeteria is being adopted. As soon as the kitchen staff can get the physical equipment needed and order the necessary ingredients, you will see that, as you suggested, health-conscious employees will be able to choose a healthful, low-calorie selection.

Your $50 reward for making a suggestion the company acts upon will be in the envelope with your next paycheck. We are always proud to acknowledge employees who help us make this an even better place to work.

The Formula

Beginning: Congratulate the employee and explain how his or her suggestion will be adopted.

Middle: Put in a good word for your organization's support of employees' ideas.

End: Thank the employee. Mention any reward.

The Makeover

Dear Aaron,

Congratulations! We are adopting your suggestion that we add a salad bar in the employee cafeteria.

    As soon as the equipment is installed, employees will be able to have a healthy salad as an accompaniment to other delicious choices or as a meal in itself.

    We pride ourselves on hiring smart employees and listening to them. Thank you for helping us make this an even better place to work. Attached is the $50 reward check for proposing an idea we adopted.

Sincerely,

Erin Nylund

Erin Nylund

EN/mj
Att: 1

Checklist

✓ Open with a short paragraph announcing the good news.

✓ Avoid redundancy. Instead of repeating *suggestion* in various forms four times, find other wording.

✓ Be accurate. Replace *healthful* with *healthy*.

✓ Be empathetic. Your kitchen staff might not appreciate the implication that until now, employees had no healthy, low-calorie choices in the cafeteria.

✓ Remember that internal public relations come into play here. You want this employee to tell coworkers about the successful suggestion so that they will give credit to the company for listening to workers.

✓ Attach the check; don't make the employee wait for it.

35

Change in Procedures

The Original

To: All Employees
From: Shawna Dupré, Human Resources
Date: [Month —, 200–]
Subject: Employee Volunteer Program

As you know, our employees are able to sign up to do Volunteer Community Service once a week over the lunch hour. The organizations we cooperate with in this effort have convinced us that we should give you more time to eat and get to your volunteer job, so that you can have a full hour to do it. Therefore, senior management has agreed to let employees take an extra half-hour for lunch on the days they do community service.

Hourly employees should stop by the HR office and get forms that you will fill out after each time you volunteer and have your supervisor sign. The form says you were volunteering and should be paid for a half hour more than appears on your time sheet. **This is very important.** No employee will be paid for that half hour unless your supervisor signs off on it and you put the form in the box on Chandra's desk in HR that is marked "Community Service Forms."

If you don't volunteer but would like to, be sure to attend the next community service recruitment meeting. They are held every six months, and you'll get a memo telling you when and where it is.

Thank you for your cooperation.

The Formula

Beginning: State what the new procedures are.
Middle: Give relevant background for the change in procedures.
End: Mention anything readers should or may do in response to the changes.

The Makeover

To: All Employees
From: Shawna Dupré, Human Resources
Date: [Month —, 200–]
Subject: Community Service Volunteer Program—Update

Employees who participate in our community service program will now have a ninety-minute lunch hour on the days that they do volunteer work. The organizations with whom we cooperate in this program contacted our senior management, who responded by revising the policy:

Employees will spend a full hour doing volunteer work and will have an additional, paid half hour for traveling to and from the volunteer job and for eating.

Hourly employees who volunteer. You need to follow these steps to ensure that your time sheets show that you should be paid for the extra half hour:

1. Pick up a packet of blank community service forms from the desk of Chandra Bernstein in HR this week.
2. Fill out a form with the date, destination, and amount of extra time (up to thirty extra minutes) that you were off property— each time you take a ninety-minute lunch hour for our community service program.
3. Sign the form and have your *supervisor sign the form.*
4. Put the completed form in the box provided for such forms, which is on Chandra's desk. Do this the same day you volunteer so your next paycheck includes the payment.

Not a volunteer? Those of you who do not volunteer in the community service program, but would like to know more about it, can attend a recruitment meeting. One will be held next month, and you will receive a memo giving the date, location, and time.

Checklist

✓ Get to the point. Announce the changes, and then explain why they are being made.

✓ Be specific. In the subject line indicate the type of volunteers and point out that this is a change in procedures.

✓ Emphasize key points. Set off typographically a summary of the new arrangement. Label the paragraphs with run-in headings.

✓ Telegraph ideas. List, using bullets, the steps you want employees to take as a result of the new arrangements.

✓ Be positive. Avoid negative language—and don't threaten employees with not being paid.

✓ Say when the next recruitment meeting for community service will be held.

✓ Be empathetic. Consider that some people find it annoying to be thanked for something they have not yet provided or done.

✓ Monitor usage. Don't capitalize *volunteer* or *community service* except when quoting the sign on Chandra's desk.

The Original

To: Sales Staff
From: Ashley
Date: [Month —, 200–]
Subject: Quotas

We're halfway through the quarter, and all of you are near or at the 50 percent mark in reaching your individual quotas, but none of you have passed your quota. Let's give the last half of the quarter whatever it takes to reach quotas. And for everyone who surpasses their quota in selling our software updates to our clients—lunch is on me at the top of the Space Needle.

The Formula
Beginning: Give the update. Rejoice or chastise.
Middle: Encourage staff to do as well or better in the future.
End: State an explicit goal and, if appropriate, offer a reward for reaching it.

The Makeover

To: Sales Staff
From: Ashley
Date: [Month —, 200–]
Subject: Quotas at Midquarter

At midquarter, we haven't reached our *team* quota. Why? Because none of you has passed the 50 percent mark on *individual* quotas, and some of you haven't even reached it. Hard to believe but true. We have superior software updates to sell and superior sales talent to draw on.

Let's make the second half of the quarter sizzle! For everyone who surpasses her or his quota, the celebration lunch at the top of the Space Needle is my treat.

Checklist

✓ Be specific. In the subject line, replace *Quotas* with *Quotas at Midquarter*.

✓ Give the news in the first paragraph and the pep talk in the second paragraph.

✓ Emphasize key points. To aid reader memory, make the first sentence in each paragraph a strong one, because people remember best what they read at the opening and the end, positions of positive emphasis.

✓ Ask a question to draw in readers.

✓ Control verbs. Watch subject-verb agreement and replace **none** *of you* **have** with **none** *of you* **has** (*none* is the singular subject and takes a singular verb).

✓ Be correct. Replace *everyone who surpasses **their** quota* with *everyone who surpasses **her or his** quota*.

The Original

To: The Staff
From: Satish
Date: [Month —, 200–]
Subject: Holiday Toy Donations

In the past, you have brought wrapped toys as holiday donations to needy children in our community. This year, please follow these guidelines:

◆ All toys should be unwrapped.

◆ Remove only the price tags but no tags that give instructions or list the materials that the toy is made up of.

◆ If you provide stuffed animals or dolls, they must be washable.

And I've been asked to tell you that childrens books will be especially appreciated for use in the new "Read to Your Child" program.

Thank you in advance for your participation in this worthwhile cause.

The Formula

Beginning: Say that instructions are being updated.
Middle: Give the new instructions.
End: Invite everyone's cooperation.

The Makeover

To: Staff
From: Satish
Date: [Month —, 200–]
Subject: Update for Holiday Toy Donations

Again this year, we are participating in the Community Toy Drive to provide toys for needy children. Our instructions are slightly different this year from past years. Please—

◆ Do not wrap your toy.
◆ Do not remove tags that give instructions or list materials.
◆ Do remove price tags.
◆ Do give only dolls and stuffed animals that are *washable* (if you give these toys).
◆ Do give children's *books*, which are especially needed this year for use in the new community-wide Read to Your Child program.

Some of you have told me that bringing in a toy for a child who might not otherwise have one adds to your holiday spirit. We encourage everyone to participate.

Checklist

✓ Add *update* to the subject line so that employees who think they know the routine and don't need to read the memo will read it.
✓ Use parallel construction for lists.
✓ Apply ego check. Where the word *I* is not required, don't use it. Concentrate on the reader.
✓ Be alert for gobbledygook. Replace *materials that the toy is made up of* with *materials in the toy*.
✓ Proofread. Replace *childrens* with *children's*.
✓ Be empathetic. Some people find it irritating to be thanked in advance; is there a better way to say this?

Clients, Customers, and Others: Announcements and Notices

Form Letter

The Original

Dear [Customer's name]:

At Mailboxes 4 U, we are expanding our services and changing our name. On June first we will become Mailboxes & More.

When you come in to pick up mail from your rented box or ship packages, you see we acquired the space next door and broke down the wall. Construction work in the new space is progressing. And you know from the signs we posted, we are putting photocopy machines in there for your convenience as well as a shipping supplies center selling paper, report covers, pens, pencils, and highlighters, labels, wrapping paper, and cards—in short, everything you need to support your mailing and shipping needs. We will even be able to send and receive faxes for you. And we'll offer more of the lager rental mailboxes that some of you have requested.

You can be sure that all the services you have enjoyed at Mailboxes 4 U will continue at Mailboxes & More as we expand into the new space in our dedication to serving you.

Sincerely,

Curtis Baytops
Owner

The Formula

Beginning: Announce the name change, giving the old and new names and the date of the change.

Middle: Explain why a new name will be adopted.

End: Assert that the name change will not affect the way you do business—or else that it reflects a positive change (whichever applies).

The Makeover

Dear [Customer's name]:

We are expanding so that we can serve you even better. On June first, *Mailboxes 4 U* will change our name to *Mailboxes & More*.
　In our added space next door, we are creating a business services center complete with

◆　Photocopiers
◆　Sales of office supplies
◆　Fax service
◆　Extra-large rental mailboxes

All the services you rely on at *Mailboxes 4 U* will continue and be enhanced at *Mailboxes & More*.

Sincerely,

Curtis Baytops
Owner

Checklist

✓　Adjust the tone. Inject enthusiasm into the opening sentence.
✓　Add empty space. Make the letter look inviting.
✓　Be empathetic. No need to describe construction that most of your customers know about.
✓　Proofread. Replace *lager* with *larger*. (Last line, middle paragraph.)
✓　For a choppy sentence, you may need to add *that*. Replace *you see we acquired* with *you see that we acquired*. Replace *signs we posted, we are* with *signs we posted that we are*.
✓　Control verbs. To convey immediacy, keep your verbs in, or as close as possible to, the present tense; in the last paragraph, replace *services you have enjoyed* with *services you enjoy*.
✓　Remember that public relations come into play here.

The Original

To: Star Restaurants Personnel and Vendors
From: John Deschamps, CEO
Date: [Month —, 200–]
Subject: Acquisition

Star Restaurants has acquired La Toque Blanche restaurant in Washington, DC, from its owners Danielle Cassidy and George Parker.

Cassidy and Parker will remain in their current positions as Master Chef and maitre d' respectively. Nothing will change except that La Toque Blanche is now under our corporate umbrella, and we expect the acquisition to further strengthen Star Restaurants' bottom line and prestige.

The Formula

Beginning: Whether this is an in-house or a public announcement (or both), give the names of the acquiring and acquired firms.

Middle: Briefly review the impact of the acquisition.

End: Emphasize the main advantages of the acquisition.

The Makeover

To: Star Restaurants Personnel and Vendors
From: John Deschamps, CEO
Date: [Month —, 200–]
Subject: Acquisition of La Toque Blanche Restaurant in Washington, D.C.

I am pleased to announce that Star Restaurants has acquired La Toque Blanche and all its assets from its owners, Master Chef Danielle Cassidy and celebrity maitre d' George Parker.

The D.C. restaurant will remain unchanged in its name, day to day operations, and personnel. Chef Cassidy and Mr. Parker will continue in their current positions. And La Toque Blanche will still feature the cuisine for which it is internationally acclaimed.

Through the acquisition, La Toque Blanche gains access to the corporate resources of Star Restaurants, and Star Restaurants expects to enjoy enhanced prestige and an even stronger bottom line.

Checklist

✓ Adjust the tone. Inject enthusiasm into the first paragraph.

✓ Be correct. Insert an essential comma after *owners* because there are only two owners and so their names are not essential to the meaning of the sentence, whereas if there were more than two owners but only two were named, then those names would affect the sentence's meaning, and commas would not bracket them.

✓ Maintain the impression of prestige by including job titles with the previous owners' names.

✓ Adjust the tone. Provide greater reassurance that the acquired restaurant will not change.

✓ Be empathetic. Explain further to readers what the acquisition means to them and to your firm.

✓ Remember that public relations come into play here.

The Original

Dear Frequent Flier:

Regional Airline and Desert Skies Airline will merge on March 22, 200– and jointly become Regional Skies Airlines, Inc.

   The merger is a response to decreased air travel in the area, which reflects a national trend. The new airline will fly the same routes that the two separate airlines have been flying. Some of these routes will be merged, allowing us to own and maintain fewer planes and to reduce the number of employees throughout the system. Such cost cutting measures strengthen our competitive position.

   Your frequent flier miles on Regional Airline and Desert Skies Airline will be transferred to Regional Skies Airlines. As a welcoming gesture, the frequent-flier miles gained on your first flight on the new airline will be doubled. We look forward to welcoming you aboard Regional Skies Airlines!

Cordially,

Byron Tripp

Byron P. Tripp
Senior Vice President
Customer Relations

BPT/du

The Formula

Beginning: Announce which companies are merging on what date, and include any name change.

Middle: Highlight the merger's advantages for the readers and for the company.

End: Encourage readers to support the new company.

The Makeover

Dear Frequent Flier on Desert Skies Airline and Regional Airline:

Desert Skies Airline and Regional Airline will merge on March 22, 200–. Our new corporate name is Regional Skies Airlines, Inc.

You will still be able to fly the same routes you have flown on the two separate airlines. However, some of these routes will be merged, allowing us to own and maintain fewer planes. We will also heighten efficiency by retaining a leaner workforce. Such cost-cutting measures strengthen our position in an increasingly competitive industry.

Regional Skies Airlines will double the number of frequent-flier miles you receive for your first flight with the new airline. And of course, the frequent flier miles you have collected on Desert Skies Airline or Regional Airline will be transferred to Regional Skies Airlines. We look forward to welcoming you aboard!

Sincerely,

Byron Tripp

Byron P. Tripp
Senior Vice President
Customer Relations

BPT/du

Checklist

✓ If the merging companies are equals, list them in alphabetical order in the salutation.

✓ Be correct. Insert a comma after the date in the first sentence, or begin a new sentence.

✓ Be positive. Instead of opening the second paragraph with negative news (decreased air travel), begin on a positive note (the same routes will be served). In fact, why remind readers of decreased air travel at all?

Benefits for
Temporary Employees

Form Letter

The Original

Dear [Client's name]:

Temps for Hire proudly announces that we now provide employee benefits for the temporary employees who we represent. Our employee benefit package includes:

◆ Paid health and dental insurance
◆ Paid vacation and holidays
◆ A 401(K) plan

You have read about the lawsuit by temporary workers claiming benefits from a large employer. With Temps for Hire, you won't end up in court, because our contract workers have benefits when they arrive in your office.

Hiring one of our temps, you know you are getting the best. We look forward to serving you when you need Temps for Hire.

Sincerely,

Jeanne Beaudouin-Hawke
President

JB-H:md

The Formula
Beginning: Reveal your new policy.
Middle: Explain how it benefits the readers.
End: Remind readers to use your services.

The Makeover

Dear [Client's name]:

Temps for Hire proudly announces that we now provide employee benefits for the temporary employees we represent. Because we can compete successfully for the most outstanding temporary contract professionals, we can be selective about whom we send to you for long-term or short-term temporary employment.

Our benefit package includes

◆ Paid health and dental insurance
◆ Paid vacation and holidays
◆ A 401(K) plan

Perhaps you have read about a lawsuit by temporary workers claiming benefits from a large employer. With Temps for Hire, you needn't worry about ending up in court, because our contract workers already have benefits when they arrive in your office.

We look forward to serving you when you need Temps for Hire.

Sincerely,

Jeanne Beaudouin-Hawke
President

JB-H:md

Checklist

✓ Be correct. Replace *who we represent* with *whom we represent*—or delete it as extraneous.
✓ Before a list, you don't need a colon after a verb or preposition.
✓ Be empathetic. Will readers who have not heard about the lawsuit feel defensive when you assume they have heard of it?

- ✓ Unless you are clairvoyant, don't give readers unqualified assurance that they won't end up in court.
- ✓ Remember that public relations come into play here. Providing benefits for temporary contract workers for whom you find employment gives you a competitive edge.

Form Letter

The Original

To Our Customers:

Glacier Fresh Water is proud to promptly deliver to your home every two weeks bottles of our safe, clean drinking water. And your continued patronage is important to us. We do, however, need to receive your payment as reliably as you receive our water.

The number of late payments has increased significantly. Beginning January 1, 200–, we will, therefore, add interest charges to invoices that remain unpaid after the due date. A finance charge of 1 percent a month, which is 12 percent a year, will be added.

If a payment is dated and postmarked before the due date but arrives after that date, interest will be charged on the outstanding balance until full payment is received. We hope this measure will help all our customers to remember to pay our invoices on time.

Sincerely,

Yasmine Tehlhami

Yasmine Tehlhami
Chief Financial Officer

YT:gc

The Formula
Beginning: Establish friendly rapport.
Middle: Explain the change in credit and why it is required.
End: Express the hope that the new measure will help all customers remember to pay promptly.

The Makeover

To Our Customers:

Introduction of Finance Charge for Past-Due Bills

Glacier Fresh Water is proud to deliver to your home every two weeks bottles of our safe, clean drinking water. And your continued patronage is important to us. We do, however, need to receive your payment as reliably as you receive our water.

The number of late payments has increased significantly. Beginning January 1, 200–, we will, therefore, *add interest charges to invoices that remain unpaid after the due date:*

> A finance charge of 1 percent a month, which is 12 percent a year, will be added. Even if a payment is dated and postmarked before the due date, if it *arrives* after the due date, interest will be charged.

We hope this measure will help all our customers remember to pay our invoices on time.

Sincerely,

Yasmine Tehlhami

Yasmine Tehlhami
Chief Financial Officer

YT:gc

PS To make paying on time easy for you, from now on, you will find a return envelope included with your monthly statement.

Checklist

✓ Monitor usage. Although the use of a split infinitive is acceptable as long as it is not split too wide, the split infinitive in the first sentence is unnecessary because *promptly* is superfluous in *to promptly deliver*.

✓ Telegraph ideas. This letter needs a quick fix. Redesign it because domestic customers cannot be counted on to read a letter from a vendor. Catch and guide the reader's eye: add a subject line, italics, an indented paragraph, and a postscript.

✓ Consider including return, self-addressed envelopes if you are not already doing so, and add that new feature as a postscript (PS) to the letter to call attention to it. (PS is written without periods.)

New Web Site

The Original

Toys at Home, the direct sales toy firm that brings educator-tested toys directly to you in your home (either individually or through at-home toy parties to which you invite your friends) now has a website where you can order toys directly, arrange to hold an at-home toy party, schedule a visit by one of our Toys at Home representatives, or get information about becoming a Toys at Home sales representative yourself.

Toys at Home toys are competitively priced. They help your child learn and grow — and have fun at the same time.

Our new address on the World Wide Web is http://www.~~.com. Please visit our Internet site and explore the possibilities it offers.

Vanessa Levin
Director of Marketing

The Formula

Beginning: Announce the new Web site.
Middle: Describe what it offers.
End: Invite readers to visit the Web site.

The Makeover

Toys at Home has a new Web site that will make your life easier. At the Web site, you can order toys online, or learn about hosting a Toys at Home party, or even sign up to be a Toys at Home representative.

Toys at Home toys are competitively priced. They help your child learn and grow and have fun, all at the same time. Toys at Home is the direct-sales toy firm that

- Brings educator-tested toys directly to you in your home;
- Rewards you with discounts for hosting a Toys at Home party for your friends in your home;
- Affords you a chance to develop a career as a Toys at Home direct sales representative;
- Provides the convenience of online ordering at our new Web site.

You can begin to explore Toys at Home right now. Just double click on http://www.~~~~~com

Vanessa Levin
Director of Marketing

Checklist
✓ If you don't capitalize *website* (first paragraph), don't capitalize *world wide web* (third paragraph).

Note: Do you or don't you capitalize *Web* and *Internet*? Is *website* one or two words? What about *on-line* versus *online*? Not all authorities agree. Be consistent, however you handle these words. The trend in electronic language seems to be toward *dot-com* (company), *Internet, online, Web site,* and *World Wide Web.*

- ✓ Announce the new Web site and its advantages in the first sentence.
- ✓ Be concise. Shorten the first sentence.
- ✓ Telegraph ideas. Using hyphens as bullet points, make a list of what Toys at Home offers.
- ✓ Give the Web site last, so it is easy for readers to click on.
- ✓ Remember that public relations come into play here. You are addressing three groups in trying to attract customers, sales representatives, and people to host home parties.

E-Mail Sent to Distribution List

The Original

I will be on vacation from December 15 until January 3, but I will be in touch by telephone and e-mail.

If you need to reach me, please contact my executive assistant Phil Wood and let him know. He will always be able to get hold of me.

Before I leave, please call if you have any questions or concerns.

Cordially,
Shama

The Formula

Beginning: Say when you will be away and whether your office will close during your absence.

Middle: Give instructions for how to contact you while you are away, or give the name of someone else to contact in your place.

End: Offer to be available, until you leave, to discuss issues that might come up during your absence.

The Makeover

I will be out of the office from December 15 until January 3, but Novatny, Poussant & Singh will remain open.

If you need to reach me, please contact my executive assistant, Phil Wood (700-444.8888 or pwood@~~~~~.com), and let him know. I will be speaking to him regularly.

In the days remaining before I leave, I'll be happy to hear from you about current or upcoming issues.

Cordially,
Shama

Checklist

✓ No need to say you will be on vacation.

✓ Be specific. If your organization will be open while you are away during the holidays, say so. And give Phil's telephone number and e-mail address.

✓ Consider whether you want clients to know that Phil can always reach you. They may pressure him to contact you when he believes the matter can wait until you call in.

✓ Be correct. If you have only one assistant, replace *assistant Phil Wood* with *assistant, Phil Wood,* . . . Add commas around a name that is not essential to the meaning of the sentence. In other words, if your only assistant is Phil Wood, then his name does not supply essential information and so is set off by commas. But if you have more than one assistant and only want clients to contact Phil Wood, then his name is essential and so is not set off with commas.

✓ Be alert for such gobbledygook as *please call if you have any questions or concerns.*

E-Mail

The Original

Rabia, I appreciate your recommending Eric Merman. I thought you'd want to know that when I called his law firm and asked for him, Andy Tobin, another lawyer there, picked up the phone and informed me that Mr. Merman recently retired and moved to a golf community in Tucson. The lawyer now handling sexual harassment cases there is Alison Rogers. We spoke briefly and made an appointment for later this week to discuss that sleezoid Tedesco. I appreciate your help and will get back to you later about whether we hire Rogers.

Whitney

The Formula

Beginning: Thank the reader for the recommendation.

Middle: Explain what happened when you followed through.

End: If appropriate, tell the reader you will provide a further update.

The Makeover

Dear Rabia,

Thank you for recommending Eric Merman. As it turns out, Mr. Merman recently retired and moved to Tucson. Alison Rogers now handles sexual harassment cases for the firm, and I have an appointment with her on Thursday to discuss the complaints against Tedesco, which, if true, are extremely unsavory.

I'll let you know if we hire Ms. Rogers. In any event, I'm most grateful for your help.

Warmly,
Whitney

Checklist

✓ Apply ego check. Whenever you can avoid starting with *I*, do.
✓ Be concise. Delete *I thought you'd want to know that* and start with *When I called*. And delete superfluous details.
✓ Be empathetic. Provide only the details that are useful to the reader.
✓ Adjust the tone. Even in an e-mail, don't refer to someone as a *sleezoid*.
✓ Be consistent. If you refer to Eric Merman as *Mr. Merman*, then refer to Alison Rogers as *Ms. Rogers*, not just *Rogers*.

E-Mail

The Original

Your computer did not arrive on the day you expected it because it was sent out by third-day delivery instead of next-day delivery, as you had been told it would be shipped. The shipping department did not get my notice to upgrade the shipping because your computer was somewhat delayed in production. Therefore, shipping will be free to you. You say that because a weekend intervened, this is now 6 days after the computer left our shipping department, and the shipper tells you that your computer does not show up on their tracking system. After your computer left our loading dock, it became the shipper's responsibility.

You have the shipper's tracking number and need to be in contact with the shipper to locate your computer. At our end, there were no problems except that shipping didn't get the updated delivery instructions in time and the computer went out third-day instead of next-day delivery. That you stayed home all day waiting for it and cancelled appointments to do so—on both the first and third days and the computer never arrived—was not the result of any communication from us. If the shipper still doesn't know where your computer is in a couple of days, contact us and we will investigate the situation, which is a lengthy process. Your best bet is to keep in touch with the shipper by phone to try to locate the computer.

The Formula

Beginning: Explain the error.

Middle: Explain the circumstances as forthrightly as organization policy allows and, if appropriate, describe how the company will make amends.

End: Suggest any next steps that should or will be taken.

E-Mail

The Makeover

My directions to upgrade the shipping of your computer from third-day to next-day delivery didn't reach the shipping department in time, and the computer was sent third-day delivery. Therefore, shipping is free to you, and I will put the refund on the credit card you used to buy the computer.

After a computer leaves our loading dock, it becomes the shipper's responsibility. But if the computer doesn't reach you by tomorrow, let me know, and I will ask our shipping department to trace it, which can be a lengthy procedure. In the meantime, continue to keep in touch with the shipper by phone about tracking and delivering your computer.

Checklist

✓ Emphasize key points. Put the explanation in the first sentence.

✓ In the next sentence, mention that you are going to absorb the shipping cost.

✓ Be concise. Indicate that you understand the problem; but don't recap all the details of the customer's complaint.

✓ Pay attention to the meaning of what you write: "The shipping department did not get my notice to upgrade the shipping because your computer was somewhat delayed in production" may *seem* to mean that the delay in production caused the failure of communication. What is *actually* meant is that "I upgraded the shipping of your computer because it was delayed in production. But the shipping department didn't get my upgrade notice before the computer had already been shipped third-day delivery."

✓ Adjust the tone. Be as sympathetic as organization policy allows. If your firm is afraid of lawsuits, its lawyers may not permit you to apologize or sympathize with the customer for fear that you would imply company responsibility it does not want to acknowledge. But do your best not to seem callous.

Short Reports

Situation: After each meeting with clients, this advertising firm distributes a memo (about what happened) to everyone who works on the account. There is no *from* line because everyone in the agency who is present contributes to a jointly composed memo that is passed from one to the next until all have had a chance to see and contribute to it. And everyone on the distribution list knows this.

Faxed to Client

The Original

To: Hiroyuki, Kim, Larry, Sue Ann, Trygve, Ginger, Hatem, Matt
Date: [Month —, 200–]
Subject: Meeting March 3, 200–, at client's office.

◆ Client will let agency know within 2 weeks if it's a go with a public service ad. Opinion is divided in client's firm: good PR of public service vs. bottom-line responsibility.

◆ Client AE green lighted black-&-white print ads for newspapers. But as to discussion about putting ads in biweekly magazines or weekly magazines or dividing budget between them in some as yet undetermined ratio, client's team will take issue to AE for decision.

◆ Clients' new logo was approved by corporate, and agency will insert it in all ads from now on and delete old logo throughout agency's system. Tomorrow Larry will messenger over camera-ready art for new logo. Ginger is responsible for getting it into all ads now in the pipeline.

◆ We will buy space for, and design a quarter-page ad for, introductory issue of *LegalEase*, new magazine for women attorneys that targets their personal lives as effected by their profession. Also, the client signed off on the *New Yorker* ad.

- Best-selling author Delilah Deneuve agreed to client's product placement in the romance novel she is writing now: will mention a different one of client's products in every chapter for amount agreed to in contract, which has been signed by all parties.

- Agency is polling college seniors around country asking them to evaluate client's products that target young adults.

The Formula

Beginning: Who was there; when, where, and why did you meet?
Middle: Group within categories the ideas discussed.
End: Close with next steps.

Faxed to Client

The Makeover

MEETING REPORT

LOGISTICS
WHO MET:
For the agency: Carla, Ginger, Hatem, Matt
For the client: Hiroyuki, Kim, Larry, Sue Ann, Trygve
When: March 3, 200–
Where: Client's office; conference room.
Why: Review status of print ads and other live issues.

ISSUES
New:
- Client considering placing a public service ad. Will decide within 2 weeks.

Resolved:
- Client AE gave green light to newspaper black & white print ads.

The Makeover, *continued*

To be dealt with:

- Client's new logo approved by corporate. Agency will insert it in all scheduled and future print ads.
- Delete old logo from all future ads.
- Concentrate magazine budget on biweekly or weekly magazines? Hiroyuki wants to cover both. Matt asked what compromises are acceptable. Client's team will discuss issue with their AE and get back to us.

PROJECTS
New:

- We will design quarter-page ad for introductory issue of *LegalEase*, new magazine for women attorneys.

Completed:

- *New Yorker* ad signed off on.
- Best-selling author Delilah Deneuve agreed to client's product placement in the romance novel she is writing: will mention a different one of client's products in every chapter for amount agreed to in contract, which has been signed by all parties.

In process:

- Agency is polling college seniors around country asking them to evaluate client's products that target young adults.

NEXT STEPS
FOR CLIENT: Larry
Assignment: Messenger over camera-ready art for new logo.
Deadline: March 4, 200–
FOR AGENCY: Ginger
Assignment: Integrate new logo in all upcoming print ads.
Deadline: March 10, 200–

Author's Note: This template is based on one that I developed for a client's meeting reports.

Checklist

✓ For the kinds of meetings that are held repeatedly, and for which written records are kept, develop a template for a meeting report that can be filled in quickly. In the Makeover, all the headings are (except the run-in headings) in a sans-serif font, such as Arial, and the notes filled in after a meeting are in a serif font, such as Times New Roman.

✓ Such memos can have a more casual tone than most business documents: They are written often and are used simply to record—in a kind of shorthand that everyone reading them understands—what happened.

✓ The writer is right not to explain the acronym AE (account executive), because everyone reading the report knows what it means. But do explain acronyms that a reader might not be familiar with (second bullet).

✓ Even such clichés as *green lighted* are okay here because these reports need only be accurate, not polished; but they should reflect well on both agency and client (second bullet).

✓ Proofread. Replace *clients'* with *client's* (third bullet).

✓ Be correct. Replace *effected* with *affected* (fourth bullet).

The Original

Dear Frank,

You asked me to report to you about the half-day workshop on e-mail that was presented here last week. What follows are the main ideas covered in the workshop.

With e-mail, access to top people has gotten much easier than it used to be. Junior people send messages to senior management that are way too casual, haven't been proofread, and waste the recipient's time with unneeded information. The tone is often inappropriate or hard to interpret. When our people communicate with clients by e-mail, we have no record of it. Confidential proprietary information, if sent by e-mail, may fall into the wrong hands. E-mail copies are also sent to too many recipients, which clogs the system and wastes the time of people on the distribution list who shouldn't be on it. Then people send responses to the entire distribution list that are only intended for the writer of the original posting and waste more time and cause more irritation.

People also get forwards at work that are not work related. These include petitions for causes, inspirational quotes, humor, political and sociological essays, etc. Even if our people only read these on their lunch hour and breaks, some of them enjoy receiving and passing along forwarded messages but others resent having to take the time to deal with them or even just to delete them unread. And people forward messages to other people here who may or may not want to get them. There's always the possibility of a virus in an attachment, too.

Employees surf the 'net for fun and do personal e-mails during work hours. Management hasn't precluded utilizing a process that would let us check on how widespread this is by reading employees' e-mails and following their tracks on the

The Original, *continued*

Internet. Another problem is that rudeness and anger in business e-mail seem more over-the-top than in face-to-face situations; at their worst, they constitute flaming.

The workshop was well attended and will be reported on in our newsletter, so these ideas will reach a lot of people and help them utilize e-mail more affectively.

Cordially,

Lori

Author's Note: A version of this Original and Makeover have been posted at my Web site, *www.writeassets.com.*

The Formula

Beginning: Announce the topic.

Middle: Place the details in an appropriate organizational scheme. (See Tactics for Organizing Ideas in Resources.)

End: Conclude with a summary.

The ideas in this letter are organized from *most to least important.* (See Tactics for Organizing Ideas in Resources.)

The Makeover

Dear Frank,

Report on Points Covered in Workshop on E-Mail Use

Introduction. The half-day workshop on effective use of e-mail, which the human resources department presented yesterday, raised a number of interesting issues. A summary follows.

Ethics. Two areas of potential conflict: (1) employees surf the Internet for pleasure and exchange personal e-mails during work hours; (2) we could read employees' e-mails and track their

Internet explorations. We need clear policies on these issues.

Confidentiality. Nothing online should be assumed to be private.

Paper trails evaporate between our people and our clients. We must have copies of these exchanges.

Organizational hierarchy is flattened out by e-mail.

- ◆ Gaining access to people at the top is sometimes too easy.
- ◆ Inappropriate or slipshod e-mails are sent to senior management that reflect negatively on the sender.

Tone is hard to communicate online and requires extra sensitivity from writers. Furthermore, rudeness, anger, and contentiousness surface more readily in e-mail than elsewhere.

Flaming is rare but offensive. An emotional, insulting e-mail constitutes verbal abuse and undermines the career of the flamer.

E-mail copies are often distributed to too many people.

Replies to e-mails may be unintentionally posted to an entire distribution list but are meant only as a reply to the author of the original posting.

Forwards fly around the Internet. Some people here enjoy receiving and forwarding these messages, but others dislike them.

Conclusion. The e-mail workshop made points worth addressing and raised a few questions that cannot yet be answered. Because our next newsletter will feature an article on the workshop, these ideas will reach many of our employees and promote more effective e-mail communication.

Cordially,

Lori

Lori Holowenzak Kraft

Checklist

✓ Telegraph ideas. Use a subject line to announce topic of the letter.

✓ You ordinarily wouldn't need to remind the reader that he asked for this report (unless you want that fact on record).

✓ Control verbs. Favor active over passive verbs: *that was presented* becomes *that our human resource department presented.*

Note: An active sentence has more energy and immediacy than a passive sentence. Passive: "Our management incentive plan *has been designed* to be integrated with our whole compensation package." Active: "Our management incentive plan *enhances* our compensation package." Passive: "An explanation *will be* forthcoming." Active: "Jane *will explain.*"

✓ Emphasize key points. To aid reader memory, restrict yourself to one major idea per paragraph: Readers remember more of what is written when a paragraph has a single dominant point.

✓ Add empty space.

✓ Be alert for gobbledygook. Replace *utilize* with *use.*

✓ Define a word like *flaming* that the reader may not know.

✓ Monitor usage. Don't confuse *affect* with *effect*: *to affect = to influence* or *to pretend*; *to effect = to accomplish*; *an effect = an influence*; *effectively = to good effect.* (Consult a dictionary for more information on usage.)

✓ Telegraph ideas. Give each paragraph a label by putting the first word or two, which should indicate the topic, in boldface. To further help readers who skim, use a vertical bulleted list and a horizontal numbered list to divide topics into subtopics.

Report to Peers

E-Mail

The Original

Dear Herb, Izzy, JuJu, Omar, and Veronique,

This is my report on what factors impact the success or failure rate of dot-com businesses. I found there are four main factors.

Adequate capital will be essential, but a steady stream of major funding will not be critical. Money will become irrelevant if the next three factors discussed are missing.

We will need excellent Website development and administration. The site should be easy for our customers to locate and get around in: the faster they can find what they want and complete their transactions, the better. Contrary to our assumptions, delivering orders to customers quickly will be less critical than enabling customers to order easily and efficiently at the site. We can count on JuJu and Herb in creating a successful site, but they will need a support staff.

What surprised me most was that throwing a lot of money at advertising a dot-com won't work. What will work is building an expanding base of satisfied customers who not only keep returning but who also tell their friends and associates about our site and products. In other words, word of mouth (not paid advertising) is the most effective marketing tool for an online business.

Cheers.
Amy

The Formula
Beginning: Announce the topic.
Middle: Place the details in an appropriate organizational scheme.
End: Conclude with a summary.

This letter is organized *procedurally*. (See Tactics for Organizing Ideas in Resources.)

E-Mail

The Makeover

Dear Herb, Izzy, JuJu, Omar, and Veronique,

DOT-COM SUCCESS AND FAILURE
By investigating what factors most influence whether a dot-com business makes it or not, with emphasis on how those factors relate to the online business we envision, I isolated four keys to success:

MANAGEMENT
First, we must have a strong management team. The six of us can provide diverse experience and skills, so we're in good shape there.

MONEY
Second, we need adequate funding. As with any business, under capitalization can be fatal. But in e-business, the importance of major funding does not seem to be critical. In fact, money can be irrelevant without the advantages discussed below.

WEB SITE
Third, we require a sophisticated and highly competent Web site developer and administrator. The site must be easy for our customers to locate and to navigate: The faster they can find what they want and complete their orders, the better. Contrary to our assumptions, delivering orders to customers quickly seems less critical than enabling customers to order easily and efficiently at the site. While we can count on JuJu and Herb's technological expertise in creating a successful site, we will need to hire a support staff.

The Makeover, *continued*

MARKETING

Finally and most surprisingly, evidence suggests that throwing a lot of money at advertising a dot-com doesn't work. What will work is building an expanding base of satisfied customers who not only keep returning but also tell their friends and associates about our site and products. In other words, word of mouth (not paid advertising) is the most effective marketing tool for an online business. And that can only be won, not purchased.

CONCLUSION

The factors sketched above in relation to our own dot-com seem, at this point, to be challenges we can meet.

Cheers.
Amy

Checklist

✓ Reject gobbledygook; use *impact* as a noun but not as a verb. Replace *what factors impact* with *what factors affect*.

✓ Emphasize key points. Give each major factor a separate paragraph and heading.

✓ Be concise. Replace *get around in* with *navigate*.

✓ Adjust the tone. Although you don't want to be indecisive, avoid making absolute statements unless sound research or experience backs them up. Revise *throwing a lot of money . . . won't work* to *evidence suggests that throwing a lot of money . . . doesn't work.*

✓ Be specific. Offer your conclusion in the last paragraph.

The Original

Dear Denny, Clarice, Fouad, Rachel, and Mike,

As you have been apprised, we've been aware for some time that some of your people are punching in and out on the time clock for their friends, which leads to the end result that we pay these individuals for time they don't actually work. In spite of the fact that stern warnings about such dishonesty were issued along with requests that employees cooperate together to end the illegal practice, in many instances the practice continued on.

In staff meetings, you formulated a recommendation that we replace our current time clocks with a newer style that reads employees' palm prints because they cannot be utilized in a dishonest fashion. Yesterday, an executive decision was made in favor of that option.

At this point in time, you don't need to take any action, owing to the fact that we are in the stage of early advance planning to set the parameters of our needs. After we get bids on a new system, your feedback will be required.

Do not advise any of the employees about this upcoming change, because such statements might have an adverse effect in that they could possibly see this as their last opportunity to cheat.

The policy of firing everyone for cause who can be proved to have punched in and out for someone else or to have had his card punched in or out by someone else continues.

Regards,

Natasha

Natasha Zinser

The Formula

Beginning: State the topic.

Middle: Place the details in an appropriate organizational scheme. (See Tactics for Organizing Ideas in Resources.)

End: End on a point you particularly want readers to remember.

This letter is organized *in chronological* order. (See Tactics for Organizing Ideas in Resources.)

The Makeover

Dear Clarice, Denny, Fouad, Mike, and Rachel,

New Time Clocks

As you know, we discovered that a few of your people occasionally punch time cards in and out for absent friends, and we end up overpaying the beneficiaries. Our stern warnings about this dishonest practice did not end it.

In staff meeting, you recommended replacing our current time clocks with a newer style that cannot be cheated because it reads employees' palm prints. Yesterday the executive committee approved your recommendation.

You needn't take any action now. After we receive proposals for a new system, we'll ask you to participate in choosing the best one for us. Please don't tell hourly employees about the new system. We will announce it just before installation begins.

Meanwhile, the policy of firing for cause anyone proved to have punched in and out for someone else, or to have had his or her card punched by someone else, will continue.

Regards,

Natasha

Natasha Zinser

Checklist

✓ List the names in the salutation in alphabetical order or by seniority.

✓ Be alert for gobbledygook.

Replace	With
as you have been apprised	*as you know*
end result	*result*
in spite of the fact that	*despite*
cooperate together	*cooperate*
continued on	*continued*
formulated a recommendation	*recommended*
utilized	*used*
at this point in time	*currently* or *now*
owing to the fact that	*because*
early advance planning	*planning*
set the parameters of our needs	*define our needs*

✓ Control verbs. Prefer active to passive verbs.

Replace	With
as you have been apprised	*as you know*
stern warnings . . . were issued	*we issued stern warnings*
an executive decision was made	*the executive committee decided*
your feedback will be required	*we will request your feedback*

✓ Adjust the tone. Soften the request not to tell employees about the new time clock yet. The practical reality that some employees found a dishonest way to increase their wages isn't cause for insulting all employees.

✓ Shun sexism. Replace *his card* with *his or her card*.

✓ Add *meanwhile* as a transitional word to introduce the last paragraph, which changes direction and discusses firing for cause. (See Transitional Words and Phrases in Resources.)

The Original

From Kathy Bergen: Call Report

October 12, 200–. I called on Coral Key Dive Shop, 1227 Causeway Blvd., #26, Coral Key, FL 33000 (Tel: 876.999.1111) and spoke to Chuck Biro, the owner and manager.

He's going to place a small order tomorrow and then if he likes our gear, he'll place a larger order in 6-8 weeks. Not just more regulators and instrument consoles but also ·BCs, masks, fins, weights. The reason is because one of his suppliers is Marquise and their regulators and instrument consoles haven't been working for him. His customers—both tourists who rent scuba equipment and local people who buy their own—complain that the regulators leak and the numbers on the instrument consoles are too small for anyone over 40 to read. So he's not going to buy from Marquise again. He thinks our line can fill that slot.

Coral Key Dive Shop is a full service shop for divers. Chuck sells and fills tanks, and wants to see our new lightweight tanks as soon as they're available. He carries the standard brands but he really likes our styles. I showed him the gear I have with me and he took some time examining it and thinking about it and comparing it to other brands. Used works like "streamlined" and "hot" and "space-age." He agreed with me that none of our competitors' gear looks as sharp as ours does.

I left our catalogue with him and pointed out we have a great record with reliability and customer satisfaction. This lead came in through our 800 number. As I said, I'll go back tomorrow for his first order!

Kathy

The Formula

Beginning: Note the name of the sales representative and the date of the sales call.

Middle: Note the prospect's name and address; the prospect's telephone, cell phone, and fax numbers; and the prospect's e-mail address.

End: Note up to seven highlights of the sales call—facts the director of sales needs to know. (You aid reader memory when you restrict yourself to no more than seven points, which is the most that people tend to remember.)

The Makeover

Sales Rep's Name: *Kathy Bergen*

Date of Call: *10/12/0–*

Prospect's Name: *Chuck Biro, owner/manager*

Address: *Coral Key Dive Shop*
1227 Causeway Blvd., #26
Coral Key, FL 33000
T: 876/999-1111
C: 555/333-8888
F: 876/000-4444
E: Chuck@~~~~.com

Source of Lead: *Chuck called our 800 number & asked for a rep to call on him.*

Highlights of Sales Call:

♦ *Chuck is getting way too many complaints from renting & buying customers that Marquise regulators leak, and their instrument consoles are hard to read.*

♦ *He's going to discontinue Marquise and sees our line as a replacement.*

- *Showed him the regulators and instrument consoles I have with me; he likes our styles and prices. Left our catalogue with him.*
- *He plans to place a small order when I go back tomorrow. He'll try our gear out on his rental and buying customers.*
- *→Wants me to call on him again in 6 weeks. If his customers like our gear (I know they will!), he'll order more, plus BCs, masks, fins, weights.*
- *→As soon as our new lightweight tanks are available, he wants to see them.*

Author's Note: This call report is based on one I developed, in consultation with the director of sales, for a client.

Checklist

✓ A sales office can adopt a template for a sales call report—such as the one used in the Makeover.

Note: A call report is a memo that can be designed in whatever format works for your office—from a template in your laptop computer, which you fill in and print later or attach to e-mail—to preprinted card stock (for example, a sheet of 8" by 11½" with up to six cards per sheet) that you fill in by hand right after a sales call. See the Makeover for a model of this style.

✓ Emphasize key points. On the call report template, make room for up to seven main points about the sales call. Our memory can generally retain up to seven points (but no more) grouped together for emphasis.

- ✓ The writer is right in writing the acronym *BC* instead of *buoyancy control device*, because scuba divers call it a BC.
- ✓ Be alert for gobbledygook. Replace *reason is because* with *reason is that* or, simply, *reason is*.
- ✓ Monitor usage. Hyphenate *full-service* shop.
- ✓ Be correct. Delete comma in *fills tanks, and wants*.
- ✓ Emphasize key points. Don't bury in the middle an important fact like Chuck's desire to see the lighter tanks when they're available. Put that on its own individual line in the list, preferably at the end, a position of positive emphasis.
- ✓ Telegraph ideas. Even if you don't use a standardized call report form, give the highlights of the sales call in a bulleted list. Mark items with an arrow → when you need to follow up on them.
- ✓ Get to the point. Resist making a call report a diary entry of a sales call.
- ✓ Be specific. Include all the information needed to follow up with this prospect.

Fax

The Original

Carolyn, here are the minutes you asked me to fax to you because you were out of town during the most recent board meeting.
Sean

Minutes of the Monthly Meeting of the Board of Directors of the Community Medical Outreach Team, August 13, 200–

Presiding: Dianne Boyd, President
Present: Irwin Blum, Liz De Carlo, Estelle Cutler, Tyrell Jones, Sean Flanagan, Lydia Khan, Elliott Littlebird, Nicki Maxwell, Sara Ofari-Mankata, and Winchell Yee
Absent: Carolyn Brown

The monthly board of directors meeting of the Community Medical Outreach Team (CMOT) was called to order by Dr. Boyd at 2 P.M. in meeting room A. The minutes of the July 15 meeting were read by Mr. Flanagan and were approved.

The first topic of discussion was the need to purchase a new autoclave for the dental clinic. Dr. Cutler, who had asked to address the meeting, reported that the autoclave only works intermittently and that she has had to turn away patients because she could not sterilize instruments. She explored the cost of purchasing an autoclave and found an acceptable model on sale because the manufacturer is discontinuing it. She needs to move fast before stock on this model runs out. The committee approved the purchase of the $2,000 autoclave, shipping included, no tax due to our nonprofit status. The money will come out of medical-equipment funds in the annual budget. Mr. Jones, treasurer, will write to major donors on our list and ask them to make contributions that will restore medical-equipment funds to a prudent level after this unexpected emergency purchase. Dr. Cutler will contact her colleagues in the dental community on the issue of donations of used but still usable equipment that could lighten the burden on this line item in future.

Mr. Yee reported that the new CMOT Alternatives to Violence training program is running into obstacles with high school boys, because even when the program convinces them to respond nonviolently to violence, many of their fathers threaten to beat them up if they act like "sissies" and don't strike back at anyone who strikes out at them. Mr. Yee said he and his counselors are looking for ways to mitigate this problem.

Ms. Ofari-Mankata reported that she has now received proof of current medical-practice insurance from all the medical personnel, which protects CMOT against any malpractice suits brought against individual medical staff members.

The group considered whether to add someone else to the bank signature card and will discuss the issue at the next meeting.

The meeting was adjourned at 3:10 P.M.

Respectfully submitted,

Sean Flanagan

Sean Flanagan, Secretary

The Formula

Beginning: Record the date and location; who met, who was absent, and whether a quorum was present; at what time the meeting was called to order and by whom; and the reading, amendment (if any), and approval of the previous meeting's minutes.

Middle: Record what was discussed, what votes were taken (note if they were unanimous or if there were dissenting votes or abstentions). Record the discussions in enough detail to create an accurate legal record of the proceedings and to demonstrate that decisions were justified. Include motions, votes, resolutions, and reports.

End: Record the time the meeting was adjourned.

Fax

Community Medical Outreach Team
Monthly Board of Directors Meeting: August 13, 200-
CMOT Clinic, Meeting Room A

Presiding: Dianne Boyd, President

Board Members Present:

Irwin Blum	Sean Flanagan
Liz De Carlo	Lydia Khan
Tyrell Jones	Nicki Maxwell

Absent: Carolyn Brown

Clinic Staff Members Present:

Estelle Cutler, dentist
Elliott Littlebird, nurse practitioner
Sara Ofari-Mankata, administrator
Winchell Yee, social worker

Quorum Present? Yes

Opening Proceedings: Dr. Boyd called the meeting to order at 2 P.M. Mr. Flanagan read the minutes of the July 15, 200– meeting; they were approved unanimously.

Dental Autoclave Replacement

Autoclave Purchase. Dr. Cutler reported that the dental autoclave in the clinic works only intermittently, and she has had to turn away patients because she could not sterilize instruments. She has called dentists in the community to ask if they could donate a used autoclave but responses were negative. She then found an acceptable model on sale, but supplies are not expected to last. Mr. Jones, treasurer, reported that there is money in the medical-equipment line item in the budget to purchase the autoclave. MOTION by Ms. De Carlo that the Board authorize Dr. Cutler to purchase the autoclave for $2,000, the sale price, which includes shipping; seconded by Ms. Maxwell; approved unanimously.

Medical Equipment Funds. After discussion about the depletion of the medical-equipment funds by the autoclave purchase, Mr. Jones agreed to write to major contributors on our donors list and ask them to contribute to restore the medical-equipment budget to a prudent level. Dr. Cutler volunteered to contact dentists in the community to request donations of used equipment whenever they replace used, but still usable, items.

Alternatives to Violence Training. Mr. Yee reported that the CMOT Alternatives to Violence training program is running into an obstacle with high school boys whose fathers threaten to beat them if anyone strikes them and they don't strike back. Mr. Yee and his counselors are looking for ways to mitigate this obstacle to promoting nonviolence. He will report further at the next Board meeting.

Proof of Current Medical-Practice Insurance. Ms. Ofari-Mankata reported that she has now received from all CMOT medical personnel proof of current medical-practice insurance—required as protection for CMOT against any malpractice suits.

Board Member Authorization to Sign Checks. The Board considered the advisability of adding another person to those authorized to sign checks for CMOT, because those who now sign may be out of town at the same time. The option will be discussed further at the next meeting.

Adjournment. The meeting was adjourned at 3:10 P.M.

Respectfully submitted,

Sean Flanagan

Sean Flanagan, Secretary

Checklist

✓ Create a template for meeting minutes; keep it in your computer and use headings that appear in all your meeting minutes: *Presiding, Board Members Present, Absent* (see Makeover for additional categories). Use a sans-serif font such as Arial for the major headings and a serif font such as Times New Roman for the minutes.

✓ Customize the template as is appropriate for your organization and in keeping with the minutes' status as a legal document.

✓ If amendments are made to the minutes, decide whether to record each one or, instead, to state simply *amended and approved*.

✓ When listing the people present, separate the members of the group required to meet from any visitors, for example, *Board Members Present* and *Others Present*.

✓ Because minutes are a legal document, don't write a personal note on them before faxing them; add a cover sheet for your explanation.

✓ Telegraph ideas. Label the proceedings with headings.

✓ Be alert for gobbledygook. Replace *unexpected emergency* with *emergency*.

✓ Capitalize *MOTION* to make motions easy to find for those who skim the minutes. Giving *Board* an initial capital letter makes it easy to spot, too.

✓ Include all germane details of what happened.

THREE
Cultivate or Give Support

Inside the Organization

Clients, Customers, and Others

Inside the Organization

Attempt to Avoid Being Laid Off

Situation: If your company is likely to downsize in the near future and you are vulnerable to being laid off, you may want to remind your supervisor now of the ways in which you are an especially valuable employee. Avoid appearing to curry favor.

The Original

To: Manny Kotzamanis, Vice President
From: Art Alvarez, Statistician
Date: [Month —, 200–]
Subject: Update on my expanding job responsibilities

My responsibilities have transpired beyond my job description to the point where my position is now a hybrid of statistics/marketing. I thought you should know I have been serving a quasi-marketing function in addition to my duties as a statistician.

In the beginning, I developed a name selection model and did mailing reprojections. I also did analyses requested by Marketing. What transpired was that Jason French in Marketing and I worked really well together and he began to come to me for advice and ideas and encourage my suggestions. His department was pleased with the ideas we cooperated on because it led to more successful marketing due to my work product targeting the prospects so precisely and my knowing how to reach them. I turned out to have a talent for marketing, and I could handle additional responsibilities in marketing along with statistics. I just seem to be able to combine them well. You could say that with me you get a two-for-the-price-of-one type employee.

Thank you for reading this update of my current situation in regard to the many job responsibilities I am able to handle.

The Formula

Beginning: Summarize the ways you contribute beyond that which is expected.

Middle: Briefly provide the particulars.

End: Imply (but don't say) that keeping you on is good for the bottom line.

The Makeover

To: Manny Kotzamanis, Vice President
From: Art Alvarez, Statistician
Date: [Month —, 200–]
Subject: Update on my expanding job responsibilities

Aspects of my job have developed over time to the point where I should record them for you: I have taken on additional responsibilities in order to cooperate as fully as possible with the marketing department.

My standard assignments include developing a name selection model, doing mailing reprojections, and providing analyses requested by the marketing department. As it turns out, a natural extension of these activities is to offer marketing suggestions based on the data I supply. It is rewarding to find my ideas accepted and acted on.

If further opportunities arise, please consider that I contribute in marketing as well as statistics and will put in whatever time and effort are required to do a good job in both areas.

Checklist

✓ Avoid redundancy. Both sentences in the first paragraph say essentially the same thing.

✓ Monitor usage. Remember that *transpire* means *come to light, be revealed.* It does not mean *happen* or *expand.* And replace *type employee* with *type of employee.*

- ✓ Resist mentioning coworkers unless you let them see and approve the memo before you send it.
- ✓ Be correct. Add a comma between *well together* and *he began*: *well together, and he began* . . . (third sentence, second paragraph).
- ✓ Instead of patting yourself on the back, just give the facts.
- ✓ Be empathetic. Give only the history that the reader needs.
- ✓ Control verbs. Keep your verbs in, or as close as possible to, the present tense. Present tense verbs convey a greater sense of immediacy than past tense verbs.
- ✓ Don't thank the reader for reading your memo. You should write only when your ideas are relevant to the reader.
- ✓ While avoiding a reference to possible downsizing, you can—in the interests of diplomacy—refer to *further opportunities* (meaning but not saying that your employer gets two employees for the price of one in you).
- ✓ Remember that internal public relations come into play here. You are trying, without seeming pushy or anxious, to position yourself in the reader's mind as an invaluable employee.

E-Mail

The Original

Dear Chang, Gilbert, June, Lindsey, Marsha, Nii, and Shamus,

Meeting federal requirements for stockbrokers' continuing education can be time consuming and takes us away from our phones and customers. We've complained about it for years. Not that it's not needed but that the process is cumbersome. I've been doing research online and discovered that we can meet the compliance requirements by taking the training electronically. We could complete the requirements on-line at home or in the office whenever we can work it in.

The best on-line courses I've been able to find are at www.~~~~~.com. Check out the site and let me know if you want to join me in proposing to Jack that we adopt online compliance training for the firm. If you want the Web sites of other online compliance training sources for brokers, let me know, and I'll send them to you.

Chris

The Formula

Beginning: Invite support for your idea or plan.

Middle: Explain why support is justified.

End: Ask readers to get in touch with you if they support your idea.

The Makeover

Dear Chang, Gilbert, June, Lindsey, Marsha, Nii, and Shamus,

We've often complained that meeting federal requirements for stockbrokers' continuing education takes us away (for significant periods of time) from our phones and customers. Doing online research, I discovered that we can meet compliance requirements by taking courses electronically. The best site I've found is http://www.~~~~~.com. Other Web sites we might consider for compliance training include http://www.~~~~~.com, http://www.~~~~~.com, and http:// www.~~~~~.com

By satisfying the requirements through online continuing education courses, we can work at our own convenience—at home, in the office, or using our laptops while traveling.

I've discussed this option with Jack. He encouraged me to find out if you all agree that this is a sound idea. Check out the sites and let me know if you want to meet to put together a proposal for Jack about adopting electronic training.

Chris

Checklist

✓ *Not that . . . but that* is unnecessarily awkward even for a sentence fragment (third sentence).

✓ Be specific. In the last sentence of the first paragraph, what does *it* refer to? Replace *can work it* in with *find time*.

✓ Be consistent. Always write *on-line* or always write *online* (first paragraph).

✓ Remember that internal public relations come into play here. Consider sending Jack a copy of this e-mail with an annotation that you want to keep him in the loop and will let him know if you get a strong response. Even better, why not discuss the idea with Jack before you solicit support?

E-Mail

The Original

Shibley, I need to take a damage control meeting with you in the near future on account of the negative quality and cost impacting the construction of the new east wing project, which is skyrocketing out of control due to the fact that COSTS KEEP GOING UP and the quality of the materials are not at all commensurate with what they ought to be for what they're costing us.

Nina

The Formula

Beginning: Indicate what the damage is.

Middle: State what you want to do about it.

End: Describe the next steps. (If you can work the beginning, middle, and end into one short paragraph, so much the better.)

The Makeover

Shibley, we need to cap spiraling costs and demand better materials on construction of the new wing. Let's discuss our strategy for getting the situation under control fast. I'll call you this afternoon for an appointment.

Nina

Checklist

✓ Be alert for gobbledygook. Replace *due to the fact that* with *because.*

✓ Be concise. Reduce the number of three- and four-syllable words.

✓ Adjust the tone. When you capitalize words in e-mail, it is generally considered the equivalent of shouting and should be avoided except for headings.

✓ Control verbs. Watch subject-verb agreement: *the quality of the materials **is** not **are***—the subject is *quality* (*quality . . . is*) not *materials.*

✓ Set a time for making an appointment.

Damage Control
for Demotion

Situation: The managing partner of a law firm has been forced to agree to a demotion for cause; he will stay on as a general partner, however, to prevent the loss of clients loyal to him and as a condition of his not suing the firm for breach of his contract. This form letter is sent to the firm's clients.

The Original

Dear [Client's name]:

A convergence of circumstances created a compelling case for the reconsideration of my having allowed myself to be persuaded three years ago, albeit reluctantly, to step up to the plate and take on the responsibilities of managing partner following upon fifteen years engaged in the work of a general partner.

In both this situation and context, it so happens that the implications thereof are that restructuring is a prerequisite of what we at Silver, Frost, Starr, & Taylor consider the most advantageous desired outcome for ourselves and our clients.

Having insisted on being released from the organizational requirements of managerial responsibilities, I will resume my preferred position of leadership as a general partner, whereas Margaret Taylor will accept the stewardship and empowerment that situational leadership entails for the managing partner.

We are confident that we can count on your enthusiastic support of the above referenced events.

Sincerely,

Miles Webster Starr

Miles Webster Starr
Managing Partner

MWS:qt

The Formula

Beginning: Prepare readers for the news.

Middle: Relegate the announcement of change to the middle, a position of minimized emphasis—presenting your new job title as an improvement for you and praising the person taking over the position you are leaving.

End: Reassure readers that the changes have only positive implications for their relationship with your firm.

The Makeover

Dear [Client's name]:

As you may remember, I was a general partner at Silver, Frost, Starr, & Taylor for fifteen years before I became the managing partner three years ago. In the past three years, I have discovered that life at the top does not suit me. It involves too much managing and not enough law. As a result, I have persuaded my colleagues to let me resume a position as general partner so that I can devote my time to clients and cases, the work I love.

Margaret Taylor has graciously agreed to take on the mantle of managing partner with its attendant duties and responsibilities. I am most grateful to her. My colleagues and I are confident that she will do a superb job.

We at Silver, Frost, Starr, & Taylor look forward to continuing our valued association with you.

Sincerely,
Miles Webster Starr

Miles Webster Starr

Managing Partner

MWS:qt

Checklist

✓ Be alert for gobbledygook. Revise the Original to eliminate the jargon that infects it throughout.

✓ Be forthright about the changes that are occurring—while casting them in the best possible light.

✓ Weed out such clichés as *step up to the plate.* If you use a cliché, have a reason for doing so. For instance, in the Makeover, *life at the top* adds a light touch to distract readers from the serious subtext (what is *not* being said in this letter is what is most important).

✓ Monitor usage. Never put yourself first. And substitute the personal pronoun *us* for the reflexive *-selves* pronoun. Then *for ourselves and our clients* will become *for our clients and us.*

✓ Be positive. Say something flattering and reassuring about your successor.

The Original

Dear Roz,

I recommend hiring, on retainer, a professional writer to edit and revise our most important documents—from one-page letters to clients to long reports. For a monthly fee, to be determined by the number of documents we agree in advance we will probably want to send him each month, he will provide us with document makeovers. I suggest we set this number at 50 pages a month. If in any given month we need less than 50 makeover pages, we get a credit and can submit that extra number of pages the next month. We can submit as many documents as we want, and if the number of pages exceeds the agreed on amount, we will pay on a per/page basis at a lower rate than if we did not have him on retainer.

I am making this recommendation because we are *competing* for the reading time of our clients and associates, and we need to be sure the firm's letters, reports, proposals, et cetera look more inviting than other reading matter landing on the same desks.

Most of our managers are good writers, but good is no longer good enough, which is why we need a professional writer on board in order to do ourselves justice. Our people are already working long hours and we need for them to concentrate on what they do best. Once managers get their ideas down on paper, the professional writer will give their ideas shape and present them in an inviting format that can compete for attention/support. I hope you agree that we need a professional writer.

All the best,

Marlene

Author's Note: This letter is a slightly altered version of a handout and overhead created for my corporate writing workshops.

The Formula

Beginning: State what you propose and why; include any relevant background information.

Middle: Organize logical, convincing details to support your proposed idea. (See Tactics for Organizing Ideas in Resources.)

End: Repeat your proposal and, if appropriate, include the next steps to be taken and any deadlines.

This letter arranges ideas (after the opening recommendation) from *least to most important.* (See Tactics for Organizing Ideas in Resources.)

An asterisk (*) in this Makeover identifies *transitional words and phrases* (but the asterisks would not appear in an actual proposal); transitions provide a connection between the ideas that precede them and those that follow. (See Transitions in Resources.)

The Makeover

Dear Roz,

HIRING A PROFESSIONAL WRITER FOR THE FIRM

WHERE WE ARE

Recommendation: *I recommend that we hire a professional writer on a retainer basis.* As you and I have discussed recently, the firm's written communications are not as impressive as they would be in the hands of a pro.

Background. The competition for our clients' and associates' reading time is fierce. Consequently,* we must be clear about our own and our readers' unspoken assumptions and intentions. Above all,* we must make certain that our letters, reports, proposals, presentations, brochures, and pamphlets are irresistible. You and I have been looking for a solution to this problem, and I think a professional writer is the best answer.

WHERE WE BELONG

Process and Cost. To create a retainer relationship with a professional writer, we will estimate how many pages we intend to put into professional form each month. Fifty seems like a reasonable number. The retainer fee will be based on that number. If, however,* we need fewer than fifty makeover pages in any month, we can submit extra pages the following month. And* if we need more than fifty makeovers in a month, we will pay on a per-page basis at a lower rate than if we did not have a retainer relationship.

Need. The documents we produce are good, but that is no longer good enough.

> In contrast,* a professional writer can make us
> look our best on paper and will free our people to
> focus on what they excel at doing.

After our executives and managers have captured their ideas in writing, the professional writer will give those ideas shape and will present them in a context that is competitive and compelling.

Conclusion. If you support the hiring of a professional writer on retainer, I'll be glad to interview candidates for you to consider.

All the best,

Marlene

Checklist
- ✓ State your topic in a subject line.
- ✓ Telegraph ideas. Outline your recommendation by summarizing the main topics in headings and subheadings.
- ✓ Be correct. Replace, *per/page basis* with *per-page basis*.
- ✓ Monitor usage. Replace *50* with *fifty*.

Note: Instead of using numerals, spell whole numbers through ninety-nine; common fractions (one-third); and any whole multiple of hundred, million, and billion (one hundred, three thousand, ten million, four billion); but 101, 2,022, and so forth.

- ✓ Monitor usage further: Write *fewer than fifty*, not *less than fifty*. (*Fewer* for number, *less* for amount: "We need *fewer* interruptions and *less* distraction.")
- ✓ Shun sexism. Eliminate references to the as-yet-unknown writer as *him* or use *her and him*.

Note: Sometimes you can avoid gender references by pluralizing: Instead of "a stockbroker keeps track of his commissions," write "stockbrokers keep track of their commissions."

- ✓ Be alert for gobbledygook: replace *in order to* with *to*.
- ✓ Insert transitional words (as illustrated in the Makeover). (See Transitions in Resources.)
- ✓ Emphasize key points. To break up a long paragraph, indent an important sentence.
- ✓ The cliché *on board* may work better in a business conversation than in writing. (Last paragraph.)
- ✓ Be empathetic. In the final paragraph, say specifically that you want the reader's support.
- ✓ How aggressive you are and whether you set a deadline for a response depends in part on whether you are writing to someone at your level or someone below or above you in the organizational hierarchy.

The Original

To: Steve Gallegos
From: Ian Blair
Date: [Month —, 200–]
Subject: Missed appointment

No excuse is adequate to explain my missing our appointment this morning to discuss my new syllabus. You generously agreed to hear my case for adding five new books that have never appeared on a syllabus at this University before as well as my reasons for dropping four books that have been included in the syllabus for my most advanced course for over a decade.

On my own behalf (and not as a defense) all I can say is that a student dropped into my office to explain that her grades have dropped off badly because she is battling severe depression and may have to drop out of school. I offered support and urged her to consult the university health clinic in addition to her doctor at home, who currently has her rather heavily medicated. I was so distressed by her pain and confusion that I completely lost track of time, and by the time I looked at my watch and rushed to your office, you had left for another appointment.

I would not ask for a second hearing for my own sake, but because I believe the changes in the syllabus that I propose are in the best interests of our students, I will call in the hopes of rescheduling. My sincere apology for not showing up.

Ian

The Formula
Beginning: Apologize but not abjectly.
Middle: Present, with dignity, any mitigating circumstances.
End: Close on a positive but suitably humble note.

The Makeover

Dear Steve,

I am sorrier than I can say that after you generously made time to discuss my syllabus—during your busiest time of the academic year—I didn't show up.

The reason is not an excuse, but you deserve to know it. I completely lost track of time when a deeply troubled student appeared in my office without an appointment, and I tried to help her. As soon as she left, I realized how late it was and dashed to your office, but you had left.

Because I believe that the syllabus changes I advocate are in the students' best interests, I will call your office in the hope of rescheduling an appointment to discuss them with you.

Remorsefully,

Ian

Checklist

✓ Be concise. Cut as much of the text as possible: stick to the apology, a brief explanation for missing the appointment, and your wish to reschedule.

✓ Monitor usage. Don't capitalize *university*.

✓ Avoid redundancy. Instead of repeating *drop* four times in various forms, find alternate wording (first two paragraphs).

✓ If you want to discuss possible overmedication of a student, doing so in a conversation rather than in a memo is a more discrete choice.

✓ Emphasize key points. Use your computer's word-count feature. The last sentence in the first paragraph has forty-eight words. The first sentence in the second paragraph has forty-four words. Instead of stringing long sentences together so that they look uninviting, vary the length. And remember that some readers look at only the first and last sentences in a paragraph.

The Original

Dear Carmen, Elliott, Justin, Kirsten, Minh, and Yvonne,

We got in under the wire because you guys are amazing engineers. You gave up sleep and had practically no personal lives in order to record in two months all the sessions scheduled for three months.

As a small token of our gratitude, I want to take you to lunch at the Couscous Café next Wednesday, July 20. We'll leave the studio at noon and walk over together and stay as long as we like—I've cleared the schedule with Anita. Please let me know ASAP if you have any conflict.

Let's hope the strike ends soon. Thanks for everything.

Ali

The Formula

Beginning: Express gratitude to deserving employees.
Middle: Extend your invitation.
End: Ask employees to answer your invitation.

The Makeover

Dear Carmen, Elliott, Justin, Kirsten, Minh, and Yvonne,

You're the best. Because of your unstinting efforts, long hours, and unflagging cooperation, Fidelity Recording Studio completed every recording session we had on the books—not only for the past two months but also for the upcoming month. The final session wound up literally one hour before the musicians' strike began (as you know all too well, Minh).

Now that the musicians' strike is here, we all need to catch our breaths. I hope you will be my guests at the Couscous Café for their lavish Near Eastern buffet. We'll leave the studio at noon, walk over together, and stay as long as we like—I've cleared the schedule with Anita.

Let's keep our fingers crossed that the rumors that this strike will be short are true. The artists who recorded during your marathon efforts to get in under the wire were impressed by your professionalism and are sure to be back.

Thanks for everything. Please let me know if you are free for lunch next Wednesday, July 20.

Ali

Checklist
- ✓ Although clichés are usually ineffective, sometimes a cliché such as *got in under the wire* conjures the image you need.
- ✓ Be empathetic. When the recipient may save the letter, it's smart to think about who else may eventually read it.
- ✓ Be specific. A slightly more formal letter that goes into more detail will be most useful to the engineers for future use.
- ✓ To avoid crossed wires, ask the engineers to let you know whether they are or are not free for lunch instead of just asking anyone with a conflict to contact you.

The many words ending in *–ing* dilute this memo's impact. To illustrate the point, *–ing* is in boldface and italics in both the Original and the Makeover (but would not be in an actual memo), so you can compare the effects.

The Original

To: All Employees
From: Scott Whitley, President
Date: [Month —, 200–]
Subject: Budgetary restraint

As some of you know, our earn***ings*** dropped 5 percent the first quarter and 8 percent more the second quarter. Projections for the third quarter are sober***ing***. At Liberty Farm Ice Cream, we have always prided ourselves on treat***ing*** our employees better than most employers do, and we are build***ing*** a loyal customer base on that principle. We are not, therefore, go***ing*** to lay people off. Instead, cuts are go***ing*** to come across the board.

Everyone here is paid more than minimum wage. Our managers have agreed that start***ing*** now, almost everyone, includ***ing*** me, will be receiv***ing*** a 10 percent salary cut for the last two quarters, which will be reviewed at the end of the year. The only exceptions are employees mak***ing*** $12 an hour, our lowest wage; we consider this a basic liv***ing*** wage. And anyone for whom a cut would take them below $12 an hour (for example, $13/hr. employees, for whom a 10 percent reduction would leave them with $11.70/hr.) will be see***ing*** their salaries reduced to $12, a percentage of less than 10 percent.

Management will also be cut*ing* costs in terms of travel*ing* and entertainment. We will be find*ing* innovative ways to do business that requires less invest*ing* in these two line items. But make no mistake. We will not be degrad*ing* the contents of our products. All dairy ingredients will continue to come from cows raised the old-fashioned way, roam*ing* free and free of hormones and antibiotics.

Our PR department is work*ing* overtime, and you soon should be see*ing* stories in the media about our attempt to trim costs without lay*ing* off workers. We expect to expand our customer base to the many people who believe in support*ing* our socially-conscious approach but who don't necessarily know we insist on these values. Our marketing department predicts their buy*ing* Liberty Farm products at first to support our principles and then stay*ing* with us because our ice cream is superior.

Unorthodox as this company-wide memo is—shar*ing*, as it does, details of our efforts to deal with declin*ing* profits—I decided that because Liberty Farm is your extended family as well as mine, your know*ing* where we stand is key to the effort we must all make together.

Let's all pitch in to produce sweeter days ahead!

The Formula

Beginning: Establish the reason that costs must be cut.

Middle: Elaborate on the ways in which they will be cut, casting these measures in as positive a light as possible.

End: Express as much confidence in the future as seems realistic.

This Makeover had significantly fewer words ending in *–ing* than the Original.

The Makeover

To: All Employees
From: Scott Whitley, President
Date: [Month —, 200–]
Subject: Budgetary restraint

The Bad News. In the first quarter, our earn*ings* dropped 5 percent, and in the second quarter, they dropped 8 percent more. Projections for the third quarter are sober*ing*. Our downturn reflects a national recession and may continue until the economy recovers.

The Good News. Liberty Farm Ice Cream is widely admired by our loyal customers as a firm that treats employees well. Accordingly, we do not plan to lay off anyone to save money. Instead, we will make cuts across the board.

Belt-Tightening Measures. Everyone here is paid more than minimum wage. Our managers have agreed that start*ing* now, almost everyone, includ*ing* me, will receive a 10 percent salary cut for the last two quarters, which will be reviewed at the end of the year. The only exceptions are

- Employees who make $12 an hour, which we regard as a basic liv*ing* wage;
- Employees whom a 10 percent reduction would take below our $12-an-hour minimum. (For example, employees who earn $13 an hour will make $12 an hour—less than a 10 percent reduction.)

Management will also cut back on travel and entertainment expenses, find*ing* innovative ways to do business that put less pressure on these two line items.

Other Actions to Promote Recovery

But make no mistake. We will not degrade the contents of our product. All dairy ingredients will continue to come from cows raised the old-fashioned way, roam*ing* free and free of hormones and antibiotics.

Our PR department is work*ing* overtime, and soon you should see stories in the media about our attempt to trim costs without lay*ing* off workers. We expect to expand our customer base to many more people who share our socially conscious values, which will strengthen our bottom line.

I share with you these details because only if everyone at Liberty Farm pitches in can we look forward to sweeter days ahead.

Checklist

✓ Monitor usage. Drastically reduce the number of words that end in *–ing,* which slow down a sentence.

✓ Telegraph ideas. Outline your ideas with headings and then group ideas under the appropriate headings; delete repetitions and digressions.

✓ Replace *lay people off* with *lay off people,* keeping both parts of *lay off* together.

✓ Adjust the tone. Delete the invidious reference to *most employers*—you're trying to take the high road here.

✓ Be correct. Replace *innovative ways to do business that **requires*** with *innovative ways to do business that **require**.* The subject of *require* is *ways* not *business* (third paragraph).

✓ Monitor usage. Don't hyphenate an *-ly* adverb modifier; replace *socially-conscious approach* with *socially conscious approach* (fourth paragraph).

✓ Remember that internal public relations come into play here. You need everyone's support.

The Original

Dear Tina,

You mentioned shortly after you moved here and took over your new position that you belonged to ASTD at the time when you lived in Albuquerque. Our local chapter is having its regular monthly dinner meeting on Thursday, November 14. The speaker's topic is a subject you raised at our last departmental meeting—how attempts to modify the organizational hierarchy affect the HR mission.

If you are free, I'd like you to be my guest at the dinner meeting at the Brighton Hotel. It begins with networking at 6:30 p.m.; dinner is at 7:00 p.m., and you choose ahead among three entrees—meat/poultry, fish, or vegetarian. The speaker will address us at about 8:00 p.m. Our customary practice is to break up approximately at 9:00 p.m. Dinner is at tables of eight and is a good chance to network. This is an opportunity to become acquainted with members of the local training community. Please let me know if you'd like to attend as my guest.

Best wishes,

Abby

The Formula
Beginning: Extend the invitation.
Middle: Explain why you are extending it.
End: Request a response.

The Makeover

Dear Tina,

Will you be my guest at the ASTD dinner meeting on Thursday, November 14? I ask you for two reasons.

First, you belonged to ASTD in Albuquerque and know its meetings provide valuable networking opportunities.

Second, Kyle Webster is the speaker. You may have read his book, *Organizational Hierarchy: Pros and Cons*. We rarely have speakers of his stature, but he is a local author. The timing is good because you have mentioned an interest in the impact on HR when an organization modifies its hierarchy.

The meeting is at the Brighton Hotel on Union Square. The schedule: 6:30, networking; 7:00, dinner; 8:00, speaker; 9:00, adjournment. Please let me know if you'd like to attend with me as my guest.

All the best,

Abby

Checklist

✓ Get to the point. End the reader's suspense about why you are writing; start with the invitation.

✓ Be alert for gobbledygook. Replace *regular monthly meeting* with *monthly meeting*.

✓ Be specific. Give the speaker's name and at least one credential.

✓ You needn't add P.M. after the numeric time of day because you have established that the events take place in the evening. But if you do write A.M. and P.M., put them in small caps.

✓ Be alert for gobbledygook. Replace *at a time when* with *when*. Replace *customary practice* with *practice*. Replace *become acquainted with* with *get to know*.

✓ Avoid modifiers that don't modify anything. Replace *this is* with *this dinner is*.

The Original

Dear Amber,

As night auditor, you are responsible for keeping the books, keeping track of the numbers—the cash drawers, receipts, and etcetera. These details all have to be correct all the time.

I am pleased to say that subsequent to our discussion last month about your errors that were increasingly wrecking havoc in our accounts, I am of the opinion that you have turned the corner on your work product. I will insert this letter in your personnel file as the followup to the warning about the attention to details and absolute accuracy that were previously lacking after you had got back from your summer vacation.

Sincerely,

Ivan Jordan

Ivan Jordan
Senior Accountant

The Formula

Beginning: Tell the employee how she or he has improved.
Middle: Elaborate with details that help the employee see ways to maintain improvements or to continue to improve.
End: Encourage the employee to carry on in a positive direction.

The Makeover

Dear Amber,

Your performance improved substantially after our discussion about the many errors you habitually made during the weeks following your vacation. Fortunately, your accounting activities have regained the accuracy that characterized your work before vacation. Good for you!

I am now satisfied that your work product is once again professional, and I will place a note to that effect in your personnel file as a follow-up to the warning you received. We rely on you to continue to perform at your current level of precision.

Sincerely,

Ivan Jordan

Ivan Jordan
Senior Accountant

Checklist
- ✓ Monitor usage. Replace *and etcetera* with *et cetera* (*et* means *and*). Replace *followup* with *follow-up*.
- ✓ Be alert for gobbledygook. Replace
  —*subsequent to our discussion* with *after we talked*
  —*your errors that were increasingly wrecking havoc with our accounts* with *serious errors in our accounts*
  —*of the opinion* with *believe*
- ✓ Weed out such clichés as *turned the corner*.
- ✓ Delete *previously* because it isn't needed.
- ✓ Be concise. Keep the letter lean, stating only necessary facts and encouraging employee to continue to improve.
- ✓ Control verbs. Watch verb tenses and replace *had got back* with *got back* (last sentence).
- ✓ End on a note of encouragement.

The Original

Dear Jorge,

Your job and paycheck are secure. You will be paid even when you are not in a position to work in view of the fact that your son's medical emergency requires your presence. And don't worry about the infant's medical bills. We will pressure the insurance company to pay all the ones they should, and we will pay the rest. And the other groundsmen will cover your shifts or we'll hire temporary help.

As for being able to afford a heart operation in Houston, if you and your doctors think that is best, Lila Gardens Apartments will make it possible. We will fly little Jaimie to Houston, and we will pay for the plane fare and hotel accommodations for you and Helen. And we will work with the health insurance folks to make sure the Houston medical bills are paid.

If there is anything else you need, let me know. We send our good wishes and will provide whatever help is needed.

Sincerely,

Calvin Patton

Calvin F. X. Patton
President

CFXP/fw

The Formula

Beginning: Reassure the employee about whatever degree of support you offer.

Middle: Describe in what ways the employee can count on you.

End: Tell the employee whom in your organization to contact during the crisis.

The Makeover

Dear Jorge,

You have been a loyal and conscientious groundsman at Lila Gardens Apartments for a decade. We are going to see you and your family through this crisis.

First, until your newborn son is out of danger, you will continue to receive your paycheck regardless of the hours you put in—even if you aren't able to get to work. The other groundsmen will cover your shift or we will hire a temporary replacement, if necessary.

Second, we are working with the health insurance people to make sure they pick up as many of the medical bills as they are supposed to. We will cover the ones they aren't obligated to pay.

Third, if you and your doctors decide it is best to fly little Jaimie to Houston for a heart operation, we will pay for the plane fare and hotel accommodations for you and Helen.

If there is anything else you need, don't hesitate to call me (772-3434).

Sincerely,

Calvin Patton

Calvin F. X. Patton
President

CFXP/fw

Checklist

✓ When your heart is in the right place, your writing can't go wrong.

✓ But be alert for gobbledygook. Replace *not in a position to* with *can't*. Replace *in view of the fact* that with *because*.

✓ Telegraph ideas. To make this letter easier to read, list in a separate paragraph each step you are going to take.

Clients, Customers, and Others

64 Networking Letter

The Original

Dear Lola,

We have a lot in common, and it was fun to share information, resources, and tales of our adventures.

I'm following up on the possibility we discussed of helping to promote each other's businesses. Brochures for my landscape design business are enclosed (with a business card stapled to each one). You suggested that some of your customers need my services, and I hope you will give those people my brochure. In the same spirit, I will happily recommend you to my clients who need an interior designer, and if you send me your brochures and business cards, I will pass them along to likely prospects as well. Such a deal!

I look forward to seeing you at next month's Network lunch if not before.

My best,

Deb

Deborah Reiss

The Formula

Beginning: If necessary, remind the reader about where you met or how you know each other.

Middle: Suggest the interests you have in common and ways in which you can be mutually helpful.

End: State or imply that you hope your relationship will continue.

The Makeover

Dear Lola,

I enjoyed sitting next to you at the Women's Network lunch yesterday. It was fun to share information, resources, and tales of our adventures.

   We discussed promoting each other's businesses, so brochures for my landscape design services are enclosed (with a business card stapled to each). You said some of your customers need my services, and I hope you will give those people my brochure. In the same spirit, I will recommend you to my clients who need an interior designer, and if you send me your brochures and business cards, I will pass them along to those prospects.

   I look forward to seeing you at next month's Network lunch.

Best,

Deb

Checklist

✓ Be empathetic. Should you refer to where you met the reader or will she remember?

✓ Be concise. Replace *helping to promote* with *promoting*.

✓ Adjust the tone. *Such a deal!* might be amusing in conversation but might not be in writing.

✓ When your name is on your letterhead, you don't need your name spelled out below the signature. The signature alone is adequate in an informal letter.

The Original

Fax to: Jaryd Sibley @ 000-587-9658
From: Dermot Kuehn
Date: [Month —, 200–]
Subject: Apology

Dear Jaryd:

Thank you for the heads-up that our fax to your London office never arrived. We have gone over the fax records and discovered the secretary who did the faxing unintentionally entered the country code for Denmark instead of the country code for the UK and made a couple of other dialing errors. The upshot was that the fax went through—to Denmark. I just faxed the document to London myself and can assure you that it went to the correct number.

    Our sincere apologies for this unfortunate incident. As you pointed out, the information in the fax was not meant for eyes outside your company and ours. While many people in Denmark read English, I don't see anything in the fax as being proprietary and feel confident the mis-sending will do no lasting harm. But that does not excuse the fax having been sent to Denmark, which is unforgivable.

    We appreciate your goodwill and guarantee our faxing SOP is being fine-tuned to prevent future errors.

Sincerely,

Dermot

Dermot Kuehn
Vice President

DK:kd

The Formula

Note: As with anything you write that may have legal implications, consider asking the appropriate lawyer to look at your response before you send it.

Beginning: Apologize for the error or event.

Middle: Explain how the mistake happened and what you are doing to prevent a recurrence.

End: Assure your reader that the unfortunate circumstance will not recur.

The Makeover

Fax to: Jaryd Sibley @ 000-587-9658
From: Dermot Kuehn
Date: [Month —, 200–]
Subject: Apology

Dear Jaryd:

Thank you for letting me know that our fax to your London office never arrived. The secretary who did the faxing unintentionally entered the country code for Denmark (45) instead of the country code for the UK (44) and made a couple of other dialing errors. The fax then went through to Denmark. Our sincere apologies for this error.

I just faxed the document to London myself and assure you that it went to the correct number.

The secretary who sent the fax to Denmark has an exemplary record except for this egregious error. We bear part of the blame because she is still shaken by a damaging fire in her apartment earlier this week. We should have insisted that she take paid time off to deal with the aftermath of that crisis.

As you pointed out, the information in the fax was not meant for eyes outside your company and ours. Many people in Denmark read English, but, luckily, nothing in the fax is proprietary, and I am confident that no lasting harm was done. Nonetheless, I am distressed by what happened.

To prevent such errors in future, we have introduced two new rules for faxing: (1) After punching in the number, compare the number on the fax screen with the one you intend to send to and make certain they are identical; (2) print a confirmation that records when and to what number the fax was sent, and attach the confirmation to the faxed document.

We appreciate your goodwill and guarantee that in the future, as in the past (with this one exception), faxes to your firm will go to your firm and your firm only.

Sincerely,

Dermot Kuehn

Vice President

DK:kd

Checklist

✓ Weed out clichés like *heads-up*, which are more suited to conversation than to writing.

✓ Control verbs. To heighten a sense of immediacy, keep verbs as close to the present tense as possible: Replace *have gone over* with *went over*.

✓ Get to the point. Don't give more details than the reader needs: Delete *we have gone over the fax records*.

✓ Pick your wording carefully—not accepting legal liability or attributing to the unfortunate occurrence more dire connotations than apply—while accepting full responsibility and apologizing adequately.

✓ Be specific. Give the country codes for Denmark (45) and the UK (44) to show how close they are to each other.

✓ Be concise. Replace *can assure you* with *assure you*.

✓ Explain diplomatically but honestly how you happen to have an employee who could make such an error.

✓ Be specific. Tell the reader how your firm is improving its faxing procedure to prevent errors in future.

✓ Be consistent. Don't say something is *unforgivable* if you expect forgiveness.

✓ Remember that public relations come into play here. You want the client to stay with your firm and speak highly of it to others.

When you look at this Original, do you feel it is so densely formatted that you would rather skip it? The Makeover is intended to look more inviting.

The Original

To: Jessica Moore
From: Chang Woo *CW*
Date: [Month —, 200–]
Subject: TWA Conference

As you know, I've been asked to speak about the use of language describing ethnicity and ethnic differences at the Technical Writers Association conference in San Jose February 23-25. To accept, I need your approval of my proposed travel budget (attached) and of CultureXploration Software being mentioned in the program in the description of my subject matter and me. As a speaker, I will not have to pay the registration fee. Last year's conference brochure is attached, so you can see the kind of publicity the firm and I will receive. I am honored to have been asked to speak and hope you agree this is good public exposure for CeXS. They want an answer within ten days, so please let me know if you support my attendance.

* * *

When we spoke, you asked me to write this memo after we talked about the conference, you wanted me to outline what I planned to say in my talk. Here are the main points I will make, embedded in what I hope will be an interesting and entertaining context:

◆ *Asian* is universally preferred to *Oriental*.

The Original, *continued*

- People with a *Latin/Spanish* background in different parts of the country have different preferences: *Hispanic* some places, *Latina/Latino* others, and *Chicano/Chicana* elsewhere.
- Not everyone agrees about *black* vs. *African American* or about *Indian* vs. *Native American*.
- It's okay to refer to *people of color*, but the only groups to which one can refer by a specific color are *blacks* and *whites*—no one refers to *browns*, *reds*, and *yellows*; to do so would be offensive, however logical.
- Capitalize both black and white or don't capitalize either word.

Whoopi Goldberg supposedly objects to any qualification before the word *American*: she is American. Period. But at CeXS, we adopt a consistent vocabulary for ethnicity: *Native Americans, Mexican Americans, Latin Americans, European Americans, African Americans, Russian Americans, Arab Americans, Asian Americans*. Some of these are divided into subgroups. Among *Asian Americans* are *Japanese Americans, Chinese Americans, Indian Americans* (from India), and so forth. Among *European Americans* are, for example, *French Americans, Irish Americans, Spanish Americans*. We have also refined *African American* to *Egyptian Americans, South African Americans, Nigerian Americans,* and so on. We sometimes refer to *Mediterranean Americans,* and many other groups, too. This is cumbersome, and some may even see it as humorous, but we believe the attempt to avoid favoring any group over another is worth serious effort.

The Formula
Beginning: State what you want support for.
Middle: Explain the advantage to the reader of supporting you.
End: Give any deadline by which you need an answer.

The Makeover

To: Jessica Moore

From: Chang Woo *CW*

Date: [Month —, 200–]

Attached: Proposed travel budget, brochure for last year's TWA conference

Subject: My invitation to speak at TWA conference

Invitation to Speak

Please let me know if you support my accepting the invitation to speak at the TWA conference in San Jose on February 23–25, 200–, and if you approve the attached travel budget. Last year's brochure (also attached) gives you a good idea of the kind of publicity CeXS and I will receive in this year's brochure and in the conference ads and program.

Overview of Speech

I'll let you see my speech after I've drafted it. Meanwhile, here is the overview you requested.

A. A survey of the various words commonly used to describe ethnic background—Hispanic, Indian, white—and of the controversies that arise around such words.

B. The rationale behind the policy adopted by CeXS: use either *American* with no modifier or *American* with a modifier that closely indicates the country of origin of the family of the person or people referred to, as in *Vietnamese American*, *Chilean American* (or *Latin American*).

Deadline for Answer

The TWA needs my answer by Friday, March 9.

Checklist

✓ Be specific. Expand on *TWA Conference* in the subject line.

✓ Add an attachment line to the heading.

✓ Get to the point. Do you need to remind the reader that you recently discussed this subject?

✓ No need to spell Technical Writers Association if your reader is familiar with the acronym.

✓ Be correct. Insert *on* after *San Jose*.

✓ Be concise. Unless your reader is unlikely to approve, you don't need to mention that the firm will not be asked to pay a registration fee for you—put that advantage in the attached budget.

✓ Give necessary details and no extraneous ones.

✓ Emphasize key points. It is a good idea to separate typographically the request for support from the overview of your speech, but use headings instead of a trio of asterisks.

✓ Be concise. Presumably, your reader is familiar with the topic you will speak on and with discussions within your company about it, so you need only indicate the general areas you will cover in your speech.

✓ Telegraph ideas. Put the deadline for a response at the end where it will be easy to spot and remember.

The Original

Dear Nicole,

I was personally saddened to read in the Journal's obituaries about your husband's passing. He sounds like a fine man, and I know you and your family will miss him sorely.

    We at The Risely Group extend our condolences. Please let me know if we can be of help in any way.

Sincerely,

Ryan

Ryan O. Spangler
Partner

ROS:wm

The Formula

Note: Sympathy letters are best written by hand, but even a warm e-mail is better than nothing.

Beginning: Express sympathy.
Middle: Offer warm personal thoughts that may comfort the reader.
End: End supportively.

The Makeover

[Month———, 200—]

Dear Nicole,

In these sad days, please accept our heartfelt condolences. Although I never met your husband, I remember your speaking warmly of him and referring to the good times you had together. His obituary in the <u>Journal</u> is impressive.

Over the years, I have come to respect you not only professionally, as an investment banker, but also personally, as a woman of strength and purpose. These qualities are assets you can depend on now.

A friend once told me that Robert Frost said, "The only way out is through." You and your family are going through a painful time. Please know that we at the Risely Group are among the many friends and colleagues who offer you support and caring.

With sympathy,

Ryan

Checklist

✓ If you can, write the letter by hand on a plain white or ivory half-sheet (a single sheet, approximately 5¾ by 7¾ inches, folded once to insert in the envelope) with your name printed or engraved at the center top in black or blue ink. Alternatively, use a correspondence card.

Note: Correspondence cards are particularly appropriate for personal notes in business. They are made of card stock and measure approximately 4¼ by 6½ inches. Your name is printed or engraved at the center top of the card; your address is printed or engraved on the envelope. Many stationery stores, catalogues, and Web sites carry correspondence cards.

- ✓ Sympathy notes are unusually difficult to write for many people, and in business, this can be even more true. The writer may need to make a determined effort to come to terms with the situation and express sympathy in a meaningful way.
- ✓ Adjust the tone. Try for a makeover that is warmer and a bit longer.
- ✓ Monitor usage. Replace *personally saddened* with *saddened*. (Can one be impersonally saddened?)
- ✓ Be correct. Don't capitalize *the* in the Risely group even though *the* is part of the name of the firm.

Praise for a Government Service

The Original

To the Park Service:

I own the Beachside Bar & Grill, which overlooks Seal Beach, and I applaud your new volunteer Seal Watch program.

As a local business owner, I was alarmed before you and some of the local folks who volunteer got Seal Watch going. The situation was getting so that tourists were going too close to the pups and their mothers, who were getting agitated. A naturalist who patronizes my establishment told me we were in danger of losing the seals, who might have moved to a more secluded location.

I realize your primary interest is in the seals' welfare and keeping the general public the legal distance away from them. But local businesses are benefiting from your efforts, too. Tourists who come to see the seals eat in my restaurant. They buy saltwater taffy and knickknacks at the shop next door. And they buy gas at the station just down the road. Without the seals, we all would have been in trouble. I want you to know we appreciate what you are doing for us as well as the seals.

Sincerely,

Bea Hinkle

The Formula
Beginning: State what it is you admire.
Middle: Explain why you admire it.
End: If others have been affected positively, too, consider including that information.

The Makeover

To the National Park Service:

I own the Beachside Bar & Grill, which overlooks Seal Beach, and on behalf of local business owners, I applaud your new volunteer Seal Watch program.

The number of tourists who visit the beach during pupping season has been growing, and people were getting too close to the seals. We were in danger of losing the seal colony, who might have fled to a more secluded location. Now your Seal Watch volunteers provide information about seals and keep the public at a safe (and legal) distance.

Tourists who come to see the seals eat in my restaurant. They buy saltwater taffy and knickknacks at the shop next door. And they buy gas at the station just down the road. Without the seals, we all would have been in trouble. We appreciate what you are doing for local businesses as well as for the seals.

Sincerely,

Bea Hinkle

Beatrice Hinkle
Proprietor

Checklist

✓ Letting people know what they are doing right is generous, and it is good for business.

✓ Be concise. Revise the second and third paragraphs.

✓ Be alert for gobbledygook. Replace *general public* with *public*.

✓ Monitor usage. Strictly speaking, it is incorrect to refer to animals as *who*, a term reserved (by the people who make and follow such rules) for people. Whether you refer to animals as *who* is a personal and, perhaps, a political choice.

E-Mail

The Original

Dear Bruno,

What a performance! You're a master of diplomacy! I didn't know what to say when Courtney insisted that she was paying the bill for lunch and planned to tip only 12% because she didn't get a bonus this year. : | AAMOF I waited tables as a summer job in college and I know how hard the work is and how poorly it pays. I always tip 20% myself, figuring I shouldn't eat in a restaurant if I cant' afford that. But I just sat there and fumed. : (You not only persuaded her to tip 20% but you also made her feel superior for doing it. :) While watching anyone manipulate a peer as smoothly as you manipulated her is not always pleasant, in this case it was a treat.

I just hope you and I are always on the same side!

CUL(8R).
Grazia

The Formula
Beginning: State what you admire.
Middle: Explain why you admire it.
End: Close with appreciation.

The Makeover

Dear Bruno,

You handled the uncomfortable situation at lunch beautifully. Because I waited tables as a summer job in college, I feel strongly about tipping at least 20 percent. But while I sat there wondering what to do, you solved the problem for all of us.

Many thanks.
Grazia

Checklist

✓ Go easy on the exclamation points.

✓ Be cautious with emoticons (e.g., smiley faces) and acronyms AAMOF (as a matter of fact) and CUL(8R) (see you later). Not everyone understands them, and not everyone who understands them appreciates them.

✓ Be empathetic. However sincerely you mean it as a compliment when you imply that the reader is a master manipulator, consider whether Bruno may find it disparaging.

✓ Monitor usage. In a letter, you would spell *percent*, but in an informal e-mail, % may be acceptable.

✓ Adjust the tone. Unless you are 100 percent certain that no one but Bruno, and certainly not Courtney, will see your e-mail, don't say anything about Courtney that you wouldn't want her to find out about. Generally, not criticizing people behind their backs is the safest course. Moreover, e-mail should never be assumed to be entirely private.

✓ Be concise. Either cut your message to make it more succinct, or break up the long paragraph into two shorter ones.

The Original

Dear Alyssa:

Your annual report is the best one yet.

First, I see that the figures infer that after a rocky past history, the basic fundamentals are stable. It's not easy for any new organization to make it, and for a nonprofit, it's even harder. Secondly, your success in attracting grants surprised me. And third, you are to be commended.

The artwork is handsome and reflects the Institute's mission. And finally, your Report from the President conveys with admirable clarity concepts that might easily have remained opaque to laymen. All in all, a first rate job.

Sincerely,

Sheila

The Formula

Beginning: Congratulate the reader on the report.
Middle: Be specific about why you like it.
End: Wish the reader success.

The Makeover

Dear Alyssa:

Your annual report is the best one yet.

First, the figures demonstrate that after a rocky start, finances are stable. It's not easy for any new organization to make it, and for a nonprofit, it's even harder.

Second, your success in attracting grants surprises even me. Commendable.

Third, the artwork is handsome and reflects the Institute's mission.

And finally, your Report from the President conveys with admirable clarity concepts that might easily remain opaque to nonprofessionals.

All in all, a first rate job. A check is attached as a modest contribution to the Institute's continuing success.

Sincerely,

Sheila

Sheila Sinsheimer

Checklist

✓ Monitor usage. Replace *infer* (*deduce*) with *imply* (*suggest*).

✓ Be alert for gobbledygook. Replace *past history* with *history*. Replace *basic fundamentals* with *fundamentals*.

✓ Monitor usage. Follow *first*, with *second*, not *secondly*.

✓ Be consistent. The subtopic labeled *third* is a continuation of the second point rather than a new point.

✓ Control verbs. Prefer active to passive verbs. Replace *you are to be commended* with *I commend you* or *you are commendable* or simply *commendable*.

✓ Shun sexism. Replace *laymen* with *laypeople* or *nonprofessionals*.

E-Mail

The Original

Dear Evelyn,

Now that corporate travel is being curtailed and your job there no longer exists, your move to customer service seems like a fine new opportunity. You've already proved your skill in dealing with internal clients as you met our travel needs and made sure we had everything required in terms of shots, papers, and currency info for foreign travel and got us the best connections and the most convenient and comfortable hotels. Now you will interface with our customers, making their lives easier and better.

But I will miss your cheerful voice and reliable input. If there is anything I can do, either in-house or in a broader sense, to help you move forward, please don't hesitate to ask me for whatever help might be useful to you.

All the best,
Chad

The Formula

Beginning: Acknowledge the circumstances in which your colleague needs support.

Middle: Express confidence in your colleague's ability to meet the new challenge.

End: Offer to help in whatever ways you can.

The Makeover

Dear Evelyn,

Although no one foresaw that corporate travel would be considerably curtailed, now that it has been, you are presented with an opportunity to do something new and interesting.

Customer service needs your tact and attention to detail. I know you'll give the same care to our customers that you have always given to your internal clients. Of course, I'll miss your cheerful voice and reliable advice, but now our customers will benefit from those assets.

If there is anything I can do, either in-house or in a broader sense, to help you advance, please don't hesitate to ask me.

All the best,
Chad

Checklist

✓ Emphasize key points. Keep the first paragraph short.

✓ Adjust the tone. Shun indecisive words: replace *seems like a fine* with *is a fine*.

✓ Be empathetic. Will *interface* and *input* sound like jargon to your reader?

✓ Monitor usage. In the first paragraph, the sentence that begins *You've already proved* comes to a natural end with *for foreign travel*. Put a period (not a comma) after *travel*, and begin the next sentence, *And you got us*.

✓ Be concise. Replace *move forward* with *advance*.

✓ This letter has three main ideas: you've been transferred; you were very good at your old job and you will be good at your new job; if I can help you, let me know. Design a format that makes them easy to spot.

Praise for Chapter President

72

E-Mail

The Original

Dear Lester,

The dinner last night of the American Society of Farming Professionals was a lot different from the dinner meetings when I first joined the chapter 5 years ago. Those meetings were attended by less than 20 people. Our speakers were our members because we couldn't attract outsiders.

I counted the people there last night. There were 45. The speaker who drove out from Duluth was worth hearing. Much of the credit for this reinvigoration of our chapter goes to you. I know you give credit to the board members, and they have been highly effective. We couldn't have done it without them, but you were the one who got us all in gear.

Here's to more of the same!

Janice

The Formula
Beginning: Express your approval.
Middle: Explain exactly why you are offering praise.
End: End with thanks or congratulations.

The Makeover

Dear Lester,

The ASFP dinner meeting yesterday demonstrated the chapter's growth since you became president two years ago.

Five years ago, fewer than twenty people attended monthly meetings, and our speakers were our members. Yesterday, forty-five of us heard a speaker who had driven out from Duluth to give us data, updates, and advice that we can put into practice.

You deserve a lot of credit for reinvigorating our chapter. Of course, you couldn't have done it without our energetic and conscientious board members, but you were the one who got us all into gear.

Many thanks for your dedication and effectiveness.

Janice

Checklist

✓ Monitor usage. Replace *less* with *fewer*. (*Fewer* for number, *less* for amount: "We need *fewer* regulations and *less* interference.")

✓ Avoid redundancy. Replace *first joined* with *joined*.

✓ Apply ego check. Instead of referring to the year you joined, refer to the year the president took office.

✓ Control verbs. Prefer active to passive verbs. Replace *those meetings were attended* with *people attended those meetings*.

✓ Emphasize key points. To aid reader memory, restrict each paragraph to one main idea. For instance, start a new paragraph when you switch to the topic of a reinvigorated chapter.

✓ Be empathetic. Instead of urging the president to greater efforts, how about ending with a simple thank you for what he has accomplished already.

The Original

Dear Senator Adams:

I am writing to express my concern over the Water Resources Board's proposal to increase water flows in the Grand River by releasing water in irrigation reservoirs. The release water is intended to coincide with downstream migration of salmon smolts, and to increase their survival during this critical period in their life history. My concern is that while data shows increased adult salmon returns from year-classes that experience high river flows during their downstream migration, there is no scientific evidence to show that the high river flows are the cause of increased adult returns three years later. High river flows are associated with years of high precipitation and snow accumulation in the mountains. High precipitation is associated with certain large-scale weather patterns that affect not only precipitation but also ocean temperatures and currents. Salmon returns are positively correlated with low ocean temperatures and coastal upwelling that results in higher nutrient levels in offshore areas, and subsequent higher productivity and food abundance for juvenile salmon entering the ocean. Thus, higher river flows are associated with an array of atmospheric and oceanographic changes that may play a larger role in salmon survival than flows themselves.

The dubious benefit of releasing water from irrigation reservoirs must be to the tangible cost of reducing the amount of water available for irrigating cropland. As we all know, our nation's farmers are undergoing tough economic times. Lowering their irrigation water will only exacerbate their problems and cause further harm to the economy of our state, given the importance of agriculture. I urge you to investigate this proposal to determine if it is in the best interests of the citizens of our region, or even the salmon resources. Salmon returns to the Grand River system in 200– are the highest on record since records were first kept in 1938. We believe that the impact of additional water releases on salmon survival and returns would be minimal, given the rapid recovery of salmon stocks associated with decadal changes in ocean conditions, and certainly not justified given the potential impact on our state's farmers and economy.

Sincerely,

Bernard Cohen

Dr. Bernard Cohen, Director
Department of Environmental Studies
State University

The Formula

Beginning: Recommend the stance you favor.

Middle: Support your recommendation with convincing, well-organized evidence. (See Tactics for Organizing Ideas in Resources.)

End: Summarize your argument and recommendation.

This letter is organized around *level of abstraction*—disproving a *generalized* idea with *specific* details. (See Tactics for Organizing Ideas in Resources.)

The Makeover

Dear Senator Adams:

I urge you to investigate the Water Resources Board's proposal to release water from irrigation reservoirs into the Grand River.

Background of Proposal. The reasoning behind the proposal is that release water would coincide with downstream migration of salmon smolts and, as a result, would increase their survival during this critical period in the salmons' life history.

Questionable Value of Proposal. Does such a release serve the best interests of the citizens of our region and of our salmon resources? For the reasons outlined below, I think not.

A. While it is true that the data indicate increased adult salmon returns from year-classes (offspring from an annual spawning of fish) that experience high river flows during their downstream migration, no scientific evidence identifies high river flows as the *cause* of increased adult returns three years later.
   1. High river flows are associated with years of high precipitation and snow accumulation in the mountains.
      a. But high precipitation, in turn, is associated with certain large-scale weather patterns that affect ocean temperatures and currents as well as precipitation.
   2. Salmon returns are positively correlated not only with high river flows during their downstream migration but also with low ocean temperatures and coastal upwelling that result in higher nutrient levels in offshore areas and in subsequent food abundance for juvenile salmon entering the ocean.

3. Thus high river flows are not an isolated factor but are associated with an array of atmospheric and oceanographic changes that may play a larger role in salmon survival than the flows themselves.

B. The dubious benefit of releasing water from irrigation reservoirs must be compared with the substantial agricultural cost of reducing the amount of water available for irrigating cropland.

1. Decreasing irrigation water will exacerbate the problems of our farmers, who are already enduring hard times and, as a result, will cause further harm to the economy of our state.

2. Salmon returns to the Grand River system this year are the highest on record since records were first kept in 1938, so their contribution to our economy is not in jeopardy.

a. Additional water releases to secure salmon survival and returns are unnecessary, given the rapid recovery of salmon stocks associated with decadal changes in ocean conditions.

Conclusion. Release of irrigation water would produce only a minimum positive impact on salmon survival and returns. In contrast, the negative impact on our state's farmers can reasonably be expected to be significant. Therefore, please oppose the Water Resources Board's proposal to release water from irrigation reservoirs into the Grand River during downstream salmon migration.

Sincerely,

Bernard Cohen

Dr. Bernard Cohen, Director
Department of Environmental Studies
State University

Checklist

✓ Be concise. Replace *I am writing to express my concern over the . . . proposal to increase . . .* with *I am seriously concerned about the . . . proposal to increase . . . .*

✓ To aid reader memory, pull out the sentence now buried in the middle of the second paragraph (the middle is a place to bury your least important points), and—with appropriate modification—make it your first sentence: the sentence in question begins *I urge you to investigate this proposal . . . .*

✓ Define terms your reader might not understand, such as *year-classes.*

✓ Ask a key question to draw in the reader.

✓ Be correct. Remove the comma after *smolts* in the second sentence.

✓ Monitor usage. Repeat a preposition rather than asking it to modify two phrases, for example, *results **in** higher nutrient levels in offshore areas and **in** subsequent higher productivity.*

✓ Emphasize key points. To present a series of complex details at various levels of importance, consider using outline style. But don't feel obligated to supply an *b.* for every *a.*

✓ Telegraph ideas. Add run-in headings to label paragraphs.

✓ To form bridges between ideas, insert transitional words and phrases, such as *as a result, while, but, thus, therefore.* (See Transitions in Resources.)

✓ Proofread. Add *compared* here: *The dubious benefit of releasing water from irrigation reservoirs must be **compared** with the tangible cost of . . . .*

✓ Avoid redundancy. Don't use *given* twice in the last paragraph but find a synonym, for example, *considering that.* Although brevity is one goal, a varied vocabulary is another.

✓ Be specific. If you are going to write *we*, explain who is included: Replace *we* with *my colleagues and I.*

✓ Emphasize key points. The last sentence is likely to be retained in the reader's memory. Use it to reassert your recommendation.

FOUR
Promote Goodwill

Inside the Organization

Clients, Customers, and Others

Inside the Organization

The **eight** references to the writer in this e-mail are in bold and the *six* references to the reader are in bold and italic. Ideally, writers concentrate more on their readers.

E-Mail

The Original

Dear Meghan,

I like ***your*** research on movies that have been popular successes after receiving lousy reviews a lot, starting with the pans of *Gone with the Wind*. **I** definitely see a fun piece here. **I'm** going to propose it at the next editorial meeting, and **I'm** sure it will get the go-ahead. **I'll** give ***your*** research to whomever is assigned to write the story. And **I'll** make sure ***you*** get a credit for research. ***You*** produced examples that astonished **me**. Remind **me** to give ***you*** more research assignments after ***your*** maternity leave.

Many thanks.
Wendi

The Formula

Beginning: Praise the employee for a job well done.

Middle: Explain why it was a good job.

End: If appropriate, suggest how the good job will improve the employee's career; at the very least, express appreciation.

Here, **two** references to the writer are balanced by *five* references to the reader.

E-Mail

The Makeover

Dear Meghan,

Your research on movies that have been popular successes after receiving negative reviews is wonderful, starting with the pans of *Gone with the Wind*.

I'm sure the piece will get the go-ahead at the next editorial meeting. And when the story appears in the magazine, *you* will get a credit for the research.

You are unusually thorough and have an excellent sense of which examples to cite. Remind **me** to give *you* more research assignments after *your* maternity leave.

Many thanks.
Wendi

Checklist

✓ Monitor usage. In the first sentence, *a lot* modifies *like* and should be close to it. *I like a lot your research* is awkward, but *I very much like your research* conveys the idea smoothly.

✓ Be empathetic. If you use *fun* as an adjective, as in *fun piece*, think about whether your reader will see this as irritating (some people do).

✓ Apply ego check. Rewrite the note to concentrate more on the reader than on yourself.

✓ Be correct. Replace *whomever* with *whoever* (*whoever* is the subject of *is*).

✓ Break up the dense paragraph into shorter paragraphs.

The Original

Dear Geraldine,

Thanks for the raise. On account of the fact that I've been having a hard time "making ends meet," this will help.

Sincerely,

Earl

The Formula

Beginning: Express thanks.

Middle: Assure reader that you will continue to do a good job.

End: Pay a compliment.

The Makeover

Dear Geraldine,

Thank you for the raise. It means a lot to me both as a needed addition to my wages and as a sign that you appreciate my work.

   I like working in the mall's management office and will continue to do my best.

Appreciatively,

Earl

Checklist

✓ Adjust the tone. *Thanks* is too casual.

✓ Be alert for gobbledygook. Replace *on account of the fact that* with *because*.

✓ Monitor usage. Don't put *making ends meet* in quotation marks.

✓ Be empathetic. It's thoughtful to come straight to the point and to keep your letter short, but let the reader know you like your job. And handwrite the note.

76

Thank-You
to Subordinate

The Original

Dear Lee,

For someone just starting out in automotive sales, you are doing an unusually good job. Two of the customers who have bought cars from you recently have told me they see fit to recommend you to their friends due to your adopting a low pressure style of sales. They had both looked at other dealers' showrooms and seen cars they liked but objected to the pressure from the sales staff. This is a community of people who know their own minds and object to being high-pressured. You have been getting the approach just right by supplying the details about the features that sell the car without trying to make up their minds for them. Keep up the good work!

Best regards,

Inez

Inez Ramirez
Senior Sales Manager

The Formula
Beginning: Express appreciation of your subordinate.
Middle: Describe what your subordinate is doing right.
End: Close with encouragement to continue in a positive vein.

The Makeover

Dear Lee,

You are doing a fine job—all the more so because this is the first time you have sold cars. Two of your recent buyers told me that because they like your low-pressure style, they will recommend you to friends. Although they had both seen cars they liked at other showrooms, high-pressure sales staffs put them off.

Our community includes many people who know their own minds and resent efforts to influence them. You describe each car's best features and then allow prospects to decide which they prefer. Your de-emphasis of selling creates an atmosphere conducive to buying. Keep up the good work!

Best regards,

Inez

Inez Ramirez
Senior Sales Manager

Checklist

Let's take these sentences one at a time (O = Original, M = Makeover):

O: "For someone just starting out in automotive sales, you are doing an unusually good job."

✓ Be empathetic: instead of qualifying your praise *(For someone . . .*), extend it without qualification:

> **M:** "You are doing a fine job—all the more so because this is the first time you have sold cars."

O: "Two of the customers who have bought cars from you recently have told me they see fit to recommend you to their friends due to your adopting a low pressure style of sales."

✓ Control verbs: for immediacy, keep them as close to the present tense as possible.

✓ Monitor usage: hyphenate *low-pressure style*.

> **M:** "Two of your recent buyers told me that because they like your low-pressure style, they will recommend you to friends."

O: "They had both looked at other dealers' showrooms and seen cars they liked but objected to the pressure from the sales staff."

✓ Be correct.

> **M:** "Although they had both seen cars they liked at other showrooms, high-pressure sales staffs put them off."

O: "This is a community of people who know their own minds and object to being high-pressured."

✓ Start a new paragraph and smooth out the sentence.

> **M:** "Our community includes many people who know their own minds and resent efforts to influence them."

O: "You have been getting the approach just right by supplying the details about the features that sell the car without trying to make up their minds for them."

✓ Strive for clarity.

> **M:** "You describe each car's best features and then allow prospects to decide which they prefer. Your de-emphasis of selling creates an atmosphere conducive to buying."

O: "Keep up the good work."

✓ A good final sentence. A thank-you letter need not necessarily contain the words *thank you*.

Notice of
Employee Benefit

The Original

To: The Staff
From: Peter Breene, Vice President, Human Resources
Date: [Month —, 200–]
Re: Discount at Ocean View Health Club

I want to be sure everyone here is informed that all employees receive a 20% discount at the Ocean View Health Club across the street from our building. I know many of you take advantage of this already, but I spoke to a new employee yesterday who had not heard.

The discount applies not only to use of the exercise equipment but to the lap pool and aerobics classes. To join with a discount, just tell them you work here.

The Formula
Beginning: Present the benefit as an advantage of working for the employer.
Middle: Give pertinent details.
End: Tell readers what, if anything, to do next.

The Makeover

To: The Staff
From: Peter Breene, Vice President, Human Resources
Re: Ocean View Health Club discount for employees
Date: [Month —, 200–]
Att: Ocean View Health Club brochure

Everyone who works for James Electronics is eligible for a 20 percent discount at Ocean View Health Club. The discount applies to the original fee and to the monthly and yearly rates. (See attached brochure for details.) This generous discount is one of many advantages of being a James employee, and what you get is tailored to your needs:

♦ You work hard, and saving time is important to you. Ocean View is right across the street from our building, and you can exercise before or after work or during your lunch hour.

♦ From time to time, your jobs can be stressful. Exercise is a good antidote for stress.

♦ Your schedules are demanding. Ocean View is open from 6 A.M. to 10 P.M.

♦ You are individualists and don't want just one way to exercise. Your discount applies not only to use of the exercise equipment but also to use of the lap pool and to enrollment in aerobics classes.

Many of you already take advantage of this enjoyable and healthy opportunity. Nothing could be easier than signing up: Just walk across the street to the health club, give them your name at the front desk, and tell them you work for James. They will give you your special James discount, and you will be able to start exercising right away.

Checklist

✓ Apply ego check. Take the focus off the writer (*I want to be sure . . . , I know . . . , I spoke . . .*) and move focus to the employees.

✓ Represent the health club discount as one of the advantages of working at James Electronics.

✓ Be empathetic. Attach an Ocean View Health Club brochure.

✓ Be positive. No need to mention that personnel forgot to inform a new employee of this benefit.

✓ Monitor usage. Spell *percent*. And pair *not only* with *but also* (not with *but* alone).

✓ Remember that internal public relations come into play here. You want employees to stay at James.

78 Cover Letter for Bonus Check

The Original

To All Hoffman Tool & Die Employees:

We have had a good year, thanks to the efforts of everyone at Hoffman Tool & Die. It seems only fair to share the rewards with those who made them possible. The holiday bonus you find in the envelope with this letter and your paycheck comes to you with our thanks and very best wishes for the holiday season and new year.

Appreciatively,

Sherman Hoffman

Sherman Hoffman
President

SH/ka
Enc.

The Formula

Beginning: Thank employees.
Middle: Point out that a bonus check is enclosed.
End: Wish employees well.

The Makeover

To Hoffman Tool & Die Employees:

Thanks to your efforts, Hoffman Tool & Die has had a good year. You deserve to share in the rewards that you helped produce, and so a holiday bonus check accompanies this letter. My family wishes your families the season's best and a new year that fulfills your most optimistic expectations.

Appreciatively,

Sherman Hoffman

Sherman Hoffman
President

SH/ka
Enc.

Checklist
✓ Be concise. In the salutation, *all* is superfluous.
✓ Avoid redundancy. Delete the second *holiday*, which is clearly implied.
✓ Adjust the tone. Be warmer.
✓ Remember that internal public relations come into play here. You are encouraging employee loyalty.

79

Notice of Colleague's Illness

The Original

To: All Personnel of Fire Station 3, Grover's Corner
From: Fire Chief Jim Giulia
Date: [Month —, 200–]
Subject: Company Commander Tony Fernandez

We are stricken by the news that Company Commander Tony Fernandez suffered a stroke on Labor Day weekend while he was presiding over a backyard barbecue for his family and friends. We pray for Tony's full recovery and for his wife Bernadette their children and grandchildren. Bernadette will appreciate hearing from you.

Company member Malachy O'Neill will take over as Company Commander for Tony while he is recuperating. Let's give Malachy our full support. He's got big boots to fill.

The Formula

Beginning: In a sympathetic tone, tell what happened and to whom.

Middle: Be sensitive in giving pertinent details and any other necessary information.

End: Suggest what readers can or should do in response to changed circumstances.

The Makeover

To: All Personnel of Fire Station 3, Grover's Corner
From: Fire Chief Jim Giulia
Date: [Month —, 200–]
Subject: Company Commander Tony Fernandez

We are all stricken by the news that Company Commander Tony Fernandez suffered a stroke on Labor Day weekend during a backyard barbecue for his family and friends. We pray for Tony's full recovery and for his wife, Bernadette, their children, and their grandchildren.

Tony is in All Saints Hospital and is not yet ready for visitors, but Bernadette needs our calls (762-9301), notes (123 Maple Drive, Grover's Corner, VT 05000), and offers of help. She will let us know when his docs allow Tony to have visitors.

In the meantime, company member Malachy O'Neill will take over as company commander for Tony while he's recuperating. Let's give Malachy our full support. He's got big boots to fill.

Checklist
✓ Be specific. Even if you think everyone knows, mention where Tony is and whether he can have visitors.
✓ Be correct. Put commas around *Bernadette*. Only if Tony had more than one wife and you wanted to distinguish Bernadette from her cowife would you omit the commas. Commas around the name indicate that it does not change the meaning of the sentence.
✓ Be specific. Give Bernadette's telephone number and address.

80

Praise for
Subordinate

E-Mail

The Original

Dear Stewart,

I did not know until I saw your picture in the paper this morning that you volunteer with Habitat for Humanity. Your work here as chief functional information systems director is so cerebral that somehow I never pictured you engaged in hard physical labor. Suffice it to say that this new view of you as handy with a hammer as well as with a computer creates farther dimensionality to your image.

I can see that working with Habitat is a good way to unwind and do some good in the process. We are proud of you.

Sincerely,
April

The Formula
Beginning: Congratulate the employee.
Middle: Say why you admire him or her.
End: Express admiration or good wishes.

The Makeover

Dear Stewart,

Your work with Habitat for Humanity, which I only learned about this morning from the newspaper, is admirable. What you do here is so cerebral that somehow I never pictured you engaged in hard physical labor, but being handy with a hammer must provide a satisfying balance for your computer expertise.

You do your family, this firm, and your community (as well as yourself) proud.

All the best,
April

Checklist
- ✓ Be concise. Delete *suffice it to say*.
- ✓ Monitor usage. Replace *farther* (refers to greater distance) with *further* (refers to greater extent).
- ✓ Be alert for gobbledygook. Replace *creates further dimensionality to your image* with *adds more dimensions to your image*. Or find a simpler way to express your thought.
- ✓ Be specific. Define *we* in *we are proud of you*.

81

Congratulations
on Promotion

E-Mail

The Original

Dear Seth,

Congratulations on your promotion from field recruiter to field manager! As one of the people you recruited, I can say with authority that you earned it. The company announcement didn't startle me but it did gratify me. And it's good news for everyone here that we work for a company that recognizes and rewards talent and hard work like yours.

If there's every anything I can do to help out as you make the transition to management, let me know.

Best regards,
Roy

The Formula

Beginning: Offer enthusiastic congratulations.

Middle: Expand on why the reader deserves the promotion; mention where you heard about it.

End: Close with good wishes or an offer of help.

The Makeover

Dear Seth,

Congratulations on your promotion from field recruiter to field manager. As one of the people you recruited, I can vouch for how deserving you are. The company announcement makes clear that the firm appreciates your talent and hard work. You set a fine example, too.

If there is anything I can do to smooth the transition to management, let me know.

Best regards,
Roy

Checklist

✓ Apply ego check. Move the spotlight a bit more surely to the reader and away from yourself.

✓ Be empathetic. *Talent and hard work **like yours*** dilutes the reader's star moment by lumping him in with others.

✓ Be correct. Insert a comma between *me* and *but* in the third sentence.

✓ Proofread. Replace *every* with *ever* in the last sentence.

82

Congratulations to Employee of the Month

The Original

To: All Employees
From: Brad Noh, Senior Vice President of Personnel
Date: [Month —, 200–]
Subject: Employee of the Month

Congratulations to Jade Gillespie in Customer Service, our Employee of the Month.

In independent follow-up interviews with our customers who have had contact with customer service, Jade received the highest ratings in her department for three months in a row. That's quite an achievement! The customers who talked with her said afterward that she helped them, she was pleasant, and she left them with a good impression of Slimstyle Kitchen Appliances. Equally important, they said they would be more likely to buy another Slimstyle Kitchen Appliance because of their positive experience when they contacted Customer Service and spoke with Jade.

Jade's name will be added to the plaque in the lobby listing Employees of the Month, and she will receive an award plaque for her desk plus a gift certificate for dinner for two at the Hunan Palace. She also gets to choose a Slimstyle Kitchen Appliance from our Employee Gift catalogue.

Thank you, Jade, for your outstanding performance in Customer Service.

The Formula

Beginning: Congratulate the employee.

Middle: Explain why the employee received the award, and list any gifts that go with it.

End: Thank the employee for the good job.

The Makeover

To: All Employees
From: Brad Noh, Senior Vice President of Personnel
Date: [Month —, 200–]
Subject: Jade Gillespie, Employee of the Month

Congratulations to Jade Gillespie in customer service! She is our Employee of the Month.

For three months in a row, Jade has had the highest rating in her department for providing customer service. In fact, customers were so satisfied with her responses to them and their problems that they said they will be more likely to buy another Slimstyle Kitchen Appliance.

Jade's name will be added to the plaque in the lobby that acknowledges Employees of the Month. And she will receive

- An award plaque for her desk,
- A gift certificate for dinner for two at the Hunan Palace, and
- Her choice of an item from the Slimstyle Kitchen Appliance Employee Gift Catalogue.

Thank you, Jade, for your outstanding contribution in customer service.

Checklist

- ✓ Add empty space. Redesign the memo so it looks easy to read. One way to do this is to make the memo shorter.
- ✓ Emphasize key points. Make Jade's name stand out more by breaking up the first sentence into two sentences.
- ✓ Be correct. Don't capitalize *customer service*. *Employee of the Month* should not, strictly speaking, have capital letters, but capitalization implies importance.
- ✓ Telegraph ideas. Use a list to make it easy for readers to skim to see what the prizes are.

E-Mail

The Original

Dear Nabil,

Your slide presentation for department heads this morning on OSHA requirements as they apply to our workplace was exactly what we needed to hear. Each slide was clear and concise. If I was paying attention, you confined each one to a single idea. And you didn't overwhelm us with bulleted points, as presenters often do. I don't think you ever used more than 6 or 7. Further, providing handouts of the summary you ended with will afford us the opportunity to check our own departments to make sure we are in compliance.

Good job!

Josie

The Formula

Beginning: Open with praise.
Middle: Elaborate on the details of the accomplishment.
End: Extend congratulations.

The Makeover

Dear Nabil,

Your presentation this morning was exactly what we needed to hear about OSHA requirements. Each slide was clear and concise, and none had more bulleted points than we could absorb. Furthermore, your handouts of the final summary will help us check our own departments to make sure we are in compliance.

Good job!

Josie

Checklist

✓ Be concise. Make your thoughts on bulleted points more succinct and tighten up your other ideas.

✓ Spell numbers: *six, seven.*

✓ Monitor usage. Replace *further* with *furthermore.*

✓ Be alert for gobbledygook. Replace *afford us the opportunity* with *give us a chance* or *help us.*

Clients, Customers, and Others

E-Mail

The Original

Dear Mark,

The adage, "It's not who you know but what you know that counts," isn't true today. I never would have been interviewed for the job at Homes-to-Go, never mind hired as manager of the architectural design department, if you hadn't encouraged them to contact me.

Not that I was unhappy at A-Plus A-Frames or looking to change jobs, but the HTG deal represents a raise, a better job title, and, better benefits. I'll call real soon to invite you to lunch.

Cordially,
Kristy

The Formula

Beginning: Gratefully review the situation you are acknowledging.

Middle: Explain why the referral means so much to you.

End: If appropriate, refer to a symbolic gesture to underline your gratitude; for example, taking your reader to lunch or dinner, sending flowers, or enclosing tickets for a sports event or concert. (Be sure this is an event the recipient would enjoy.)

The Makeover

Dear Mark,

If it weren't for you, no one at Homes to Go would have thought of me when they needed a new manager of the architectural design department, because they thought I could never be lured away from A-Plus A-Frames. But these days, it's not just what you know—whom you know is at least as important. And I know you, one of the most skilled networkers in the Northwest.

Many thanks for suggesting to Stan that he see if I would be interested in leaving A-Plus for the better HTG assignment. The new job gives a considerable boost to my career.

As soon as this hectic transition is accomplished, I'll take you to lunch at your favorite restaurant.

Cordially,
Kristy

Checklist

✓ *Be correct.* Replace *who* with *whom* (*whom* is the object of *know*).
✓ Apply ego check. Spotlight your reader, who made the referral, and outline the positive results.
✓ Be specific. Sketch the details of who interviewed you and why you accepted the job offer.
✓ Be empathetic. Let the reader know why you haven't yet called for lunch.

Thank-You
to Customer

The Original

Dear Mrs. Vanderwicken:

Thank you for returning the insurance money you collected when you lost your diamond engagement ring. Many people, if a relative found a valuable ring that was lost, would not return the money they had received back to the insurance company.

As you have discovered, your engagement ring is worth considerably more than when you insured it. May I suggest that you have it appraised and that we insure it for its current worth?

Sincerely,

Richard G. Huey

Richard G. Huey
President

RGH:dk-b

The Formula

Beginning: Thank the customer.

Middle: Expand on your gratitude to, and appreciation of, the customer.

End: Wish the customer well.

The Makeover

Dear Mrs. Vanderwicken:

There are few happy surprises in the insurance business, but your letter and check brought me a happy surprise today. I am delighted that your son-in-law found your diamond engagement ring after you thought you had lost it and had collected the insurance.

But even more than the money you returned, the fact that you did return it out of a sense of personal honor fills me with admiration. Many thanks. May you continue to enjoy your engagement ring for many more years.

Sincerely,

Richard G. Huey

Richard G. Huey
President

RGH:dk-b

Checklist
- ✓ Adjust the tone. Take the time to write a glowing thank-you letter.
- ✓ Create a clear order. Replace "Many people, if a relative found a valuable ring that was lost, would not return the money they had received back to the insurance company" with "Having received insurance money for a lost engagement ring, many people would not return the money when the ring was found."
- ✓ Be empathetic. Don't try to sell a customer something in a goodwill letter. Write a second letter for the attempted sales.

The Original

Dear Mia,

I remember your once mentioning that you spent your honeymoon in Hawaii at Whale's Tail Cove. That's why I'm passing along to you these two passes for a screening of "The Hibiscus Heist," which was filmed on location in Hawaii, principally at that resort. They will admit you and a guest to the screening room on W. 52 St. All the details are on the passes. You're such a big movie fan that I hope this flick is fun. The buzz is that it'll be a hit. If you can't make it, please don't give the passes to anyone else.

Have fun.

Gail

Gail McFie
Executive Editor

GM:ye

The Formula
Beginning: Announce the favor.
Middle: Supply details.
End: Express goodwill.

The Makeover

Dear Mia,

Here are the two passes we discussed. The time and place for the screening of *The Hibiscus Heist* are on the passes. Because the film was shot in Hawaii, mainly at Whale's Tail Cove, where you spent your honeymoon, I'll be interested to hear your take on it.

The buzz is that the film will be a hit. I hope it's a hit with you.

Have fun.

Gail

Gail McFie
Executive Editor

GM:ye

Checklist

✓ Apply ego check. Don't start with *I* if you can avoid it.
✓ Get to the point at the opening.
✓ Put a film name in italics not quotation marks.
✓ If the details are on the passes, you needn't mention that the screening room is on West 52nd Street (but spell street if you do mention it).
✓ Be empathetic. Instead of injecting a negative note, telephone Mia and ask if she wants the passes before sending them to her.

87

Support for
New Business

The Original

Dear Ms. Rosas and Ms. Sharif:

Congratulations on the grand opening of your new store, The Source for Pets.

As a kennel owner, I particularly want to acknowledge what a fine thing you are doing by cooperating with local veterinarians in giving discount coupons for spaying and neutering during your opening week. Those of us who offer fine dogs (and cats) for sale are particularly upset by the numbers of animals who end up in the animal shelter, not all of whom find homes.

I will recommend your store to my customers.

Sincerely,

Cory West

Cory West

The Formula

Beginning: Express support for the new business.

Middle: Explain why you welcome it.

End: Offer any support you can.

The Makeover

Dear Ms. Rosas and Ms. Sharif:

Congratulations on the opening of your new pet store, which is a welcome addition to our community.

As a kennel owner, I appreciate your cooperation with local veterinarians in giving customers spaying and neutering discount coupons during your opening week. Those of us who are professionally involved with pets are particularly aware of the number of animals who end up in the animal shelter, not all of whom find homes.

I look forward to meeting you when I come in to buy supplies for my kennel. And I will recommend your store to my customers.

Sincerely,

Cory West

Ms. Cory West

Checklist

✓ Be empathetic. The owners know the name of their new store.

✓ As a business owner in town yourself, extend a welcome.

✓ Instead of saying you want to acknowledge what the readers are doing, just acknowledge it.

✓ Create a clear order. Reposition *spaying and neutering* so an inference can't be made that the surgery must be done during opening week.

✓ Be specific. If only customers (and not browsers) get the coupons, mention that.

✓ If you plan to patronize the store, say so.

✓ For an androgynous name, include (Ms.) or (Mr.) before it.

88

Cover Letter
for Clipping

One way to keep in touch with a client, customer, or colleague without actually doing business is to send a clipping on a subject of interest to the reader. The topic may be business related but need not be.

The Original

Dear Twahir,

The enclosed *Times* article expands on a subject we discussed at lunch last week—the ratio of the CEO's salary to that of the lowest paid worker. Although it doesn't raise the questions we couldn't answer—can and should a board try to convince an outstanding leader to accept a comparatively modest compensation package in order to pay hourly workers better—it does give some excellent insights into how CEOs think about their compensation packages and about their low-wage employees.

My best,

Theo

The Formula

Beginning: Mention the subject of the enclosed clipping.
Middle: Add a personal thought on the subject.
End: Close cordially.

The Makeover

Dear Twahir,

Was a *Times* reporter eavesdropping from the next table when we had lunch last week—or is it just a coincidence that the enclosed article from today's edition expands on a subject we discussed at length?

The piece doesn't raise the questions we couldn't answer about whether a board should try to convince an outstanding leader to accept a relatively modest compensation package to offset paying workers better. But the writer delivers useful insights into how CEOs think about their compensation packages and about their low-wage employees.

It was great to see you and get caught up on the news from your coast.

My best,

Theo

Checklist

✓ Be empathetic. Will the reader remember without being told that the topic is one that you and he have discussed?

✓ Be concise. Break up the long, second sentence into shorter ones. And delete extraneous words.

✓ Adjust the tone. Add a friendly note at the end.

The Original

Dear Ken,

Is my face red! I can't believe I sent you a bottle of champagne as recognition of your winning the HYA Videoconferencing Technology account. I know you've been on the wagon for years. I must have had a senior moment when I selected my favorite champagne for you. You worked hard for that account and deserved to get it, which is what I was trying to say.

Please forgive my faux pas and let me take you to lunch.

Cordially,

Sandy

The Formula

Beginning: Extend an apology.

Middle: Explain the circumstances without making them sound like an excuse.

End: Hold out an olive branch.

The Makeover

Dear Ken,

What a gaffe sending you a bottle of champagne was. I must have had a senior moment when I chose that gift as a token of my respect for your winning the HYA Videoconferencing Technology account. My intended message was that you worked hard for the account and deserve to celebrate it.

Please forgive my faux pas and let me take you to lunch. I will call you when I get back from Chicago at the end of the week. You will probably tell me I should hold videoconferences instead of traveling to meetings, and I look forward to that conversation.

Cordially,

Sandy

Checklist

✓ Weed out such clichés as *is my face red.*
✓ Apply ego check. Mention yourself less often.
✓ Be empathetic. Ken will realize without your saying it that you remember now that he doesn't drink alcohol.
✓ Be specific. Tell Ken when you will contact him to make a lunch date.
✓ Adjust the tone. Consider handwriting the apology on a correspondence card, which is a personal touch. (See note on correspondence cards in the Checklist for #67.)

Defense of Price Increases

The Original

Dear Antonio:

I sympathize with your wish that we had not raised prices. We put it off as long as we could. In order to stay in business, we finally had to pass along to our customers some of the increased costs we ourselves are experiencing.

For example, our furniture is made of solid wood, and the cost of raw lumber is increasing, in part because there is not an endless supply of forests to supply lumber and partly because the price of gas keeps going up and makes shipping lumber to our factories and shipping our furniture to our clients more costly.

We kept the price increase as modest as we reasonably could. One way you might lessen the impact would be to order more pieces at one time so that you would receive a bulk discount. You might also want to carry more of our lighter-weight, contemporary styles because they cost less to make and ship. Importantly, we believe your customers will be willing to pay for the high quality we provide, and hopefully, you can pass along to them some or all of our recent price increases.

We appreciate your business and know our success depends on your success with our line. Please call if you have any further questions or concerns.

Sincerely,

Elaine

Elaine Gluck
Vice President

EG/ph

The Formula

Beginning: Thank your customer for opening a dialogue with you on the subject.

Middle: Explain why you raised prices; suggest ways your customer can minimize the impact.

End: Invite a telephone call; express appreciation for your customer's business.

The Makeover

Dear Antonio:

Thank you for writing to me about our recent price increases. Like you, I wish we were able to continue with our former price schedule. But to stay in business, we have to pass along to our customers some of the higher costs we are experiencing.

Explanation. We put off price increases as long as we could and kept them as modest as possible, considering that our furniture is made of solid wood, and the cost of raw lumber is rising because the supply is limited. Moreover, as the price of gas goes up nationally, so do the costs both for shipping lumber to our factories and for shipping furniture from our factories to our customers.

Suggestions. You are a good customer, and we want to help you in whatever ways we can. Here are a few ideas:

♦ Can you order more pieces at one time and receive a bulk discount?

♦ How about carrying more of our lightweight, contemporary styles? They cost less to make and to ship.

♦ Are you passing along the price increases to your customers? We believe furniture buyers are willing to pay more for the high quality we provide.

Please call me if you want to discuss these—or other—ideas about how best to absorb price increases. We appreciate your business and recognize that our success depends on your success.

Sincerely,

Elaine

Elaine Gluck
Vice President

EG/ph

Checklist

✓ Apply ego check. Make the first sentence about the customer, not about you.

✓ Telegraph ideas. Use run-in headings to tell the reader at first glance that you are supplying both an explanation for price increases and suggestions for how to deal with them.

✓ Monitor usage. Don't pair *in part* with *partly*—choose one (second paragraph). Replace *importantly* with *most important* (third paragraph).

✓ Be empathetic. Is your reader one of the people whose hair stands on end when *hopefully* is used to mean *I hope* or *we hope* instead of *in a hopeful way*? (Last sentence, third paragraph.)

✓ Insert a question to elicit greater reader participation. We respond automatically to questions.

✓ Be alert for gobbledygook. Replace *please call if you have any further questions or concerns.*

✓ Remember that public relations come into play here. You want the customer to continue to buy your furniture.

The Original

Dear Mrs. Weinberg:

Please accept with my complements the enclosed clothes steamer, which replaces the one that you bought from us yesterday and that broke the first time you used it. As president of Hampton-Yost Housewares, I make it a policy to answer my own telephone from time to time instead of waiting for a secretary to answer—just to be sure I stay in touch with what's going on.

Today you were on the line and you told me you had intended to present your problem to my executive assistant. I trust she would have dealt with it as swiftly as I now do by messengering over a replacement steamer to your apartment. A problem like yours is not the kind we run into very often, but when we do we want to solve it immediately.

I enjoyed talking to you. Thank you for patronizing Hampton-Yost. We look forward to many more years of serving your housewares needs.

Sincerely,

Duncan Lum

Duncan Lum
President

DL:ki
By messenger: clothes steamer

The Formula
Beginning: Acknowledge the customer's complaint.
Middle: Describe how you will satisfy the customer.
End: Thank the customer for the business and offer assurances of your organization's reliability.

The Makeover

Dear Mrs. Weinberg:

Please accept with my compliments the enclosed clothes steamer, which replaces the faulty one that you bought at Hampton-Yost yesterday.

Our merchandise is of the finest quality. When a problem like yours arises, it is a fluke, and we put it right immediately. That's why I'm sending the new steamer to your apartment by messenger.

It was a pleasure to talk with you, a longtime and loyal Hampton-Yost customer. Thank you for calling. We look forward to many more years of supplying you with reliable products and friendly service.

Sincerely,

Duncan Lum

Duncan Lum
President

DL:ki
By messenger: clothes steamer

Checklist

✓ Get to the point. Mrs. Weinberg doesn't need your mini-autobiography. Stick to (a) her steamer problem and (b) the reliability of Hampton-Yost.

✓ Be correct. Beware of homophones—words that sound the same but are spelled differently. Replace *complements* with *compliments* (first paragraph). A simple way to remember the difference is that a compliment flatters the ego or *I*, and it is spelled with *li* not *le*.

✓ Be concise. Don't review the customer's call; she knows what was said.

✓ Be correct. In the first sentence of the middle paragraph, add a comma here: *on the line, and you.* . . . . In the last sentence of the middle paragraph, add a comma here: *when we do, we want* . . . .

✓ Language purists may want you to substitute *such as* for *like* in *problem like yours* (middle paragraph), but *such as* is given as a synonym for *like* in more than one standard dictionary, and to substitute six letters and a space for a correct four-letter word is to stray in the direction of gobbledygook. Alternating *like* and *such as,* however, provides variety.

✓ Consider saying that you enjoyed *talking* **with** her, which sounds more inclusive than *talking to* (last paragraph).

✓ Remember that public relations come into play here. You are fishing for positive word-of-mouth recommendations as well as continued patronage.

Welcome to
New Customer

The **nine** references to the writer and the writer's organization in this form letter are in bold as are the *two* references to the reader, also in italics. Ideally, writers concentrate more on their readers.

The Original

Dear [Fill in name]:

Thank *you* for opening a checking account with **Century Bank & Trust. We** have been a trusted member of the community for over a century.

We meet a wide range of financial needs. For example, beside checking accounts, **we** offer savings accounts, rental safe deposit boxes, and CDs. In addition, **we** provide home mortgages and home equity loans. **We** also are the source for personal loans and credit lines. And customers rely on **us** for online banking, ATM/check cards and credit cards. These are only a small number of the many advantages **we** extend.

We are here for *you,* whatever the banking situation.

Cordially,

Julia Amusson

Julia Amusson
President

JA:wf

The Formula

Beginning: Welcome the customer, indicating the reason (e.g., opened checking account).

Middle: Sketch any other services you can provide.

End: Reassure the customer that choosing you was wise.

Here, **ten** references to the writer and the writer's organization are balanced by *ten* references to the reader.

The Makeover

Dear [Fill in name]:

Welcome to **Century Bank & Trust.** *You* made a wise choice when *you* opened a checking account with **us** because **we** have met the test of time. Some of **our** customers' families have been with **us** from generation to generation, for as long as a century. **We** hope this is the beginning of a long-lasting relationship with *you,* too.

You can rely on **us** for a wide range of financial needs. For example, in addition to checking accounts, *you* may choose

- ◆ Savings accounts
- ◆ Safe deposit boxes
- ◆ Certificates of deposit (CDs)
- ◆ Electronic transfers of money and online banking
- ◆ ATM, check cards, and credit cards
- ◆ Student financial services
- ◆ Home mortgages and home equity loans
- ◆ Personal loans, credit lines, and auto financing

Our personal bankers are available for consultation whenever *you* are ready to discuss *your* financial requirements.

Thank *you* for *your* business. **We** will strive to justify *your* confidence in **us.**

Cordially,

Julia Amusson

Julia Amusson
President

JA:wf

Checklist

✓ Apply ego check. Redress the balance of *we*'s and *you*'s.

✓ Telegraph ideas. To help your reader quickly grasp your wide range of banking products and services, put these features in a bulleted list. The list format also allows you to mention more features and, at the same time, to achieve brevity. (Setting each feature in the context of a sentence makes the letter too long.)

✓ Monitor usage. Replace *beside* (which means *close to*) with *besides* (which means *in addition to*). (Second paragraph.)

✓ Be alert for gobbledygook. Substitute *few* for *small number of* (second paragraph).

✓ Weed out such clichés as *we are here for you* (third paragraph).

✓ Remember that public relations come into play here. You want the customer to take advantage of your other services and products.

The Original

Dear Birgit,

I thought your acceptance speech last night for the Business Woman of the Year award was terrific. And the recognition is well-deserved. As a meeting planner, you have a national reputation for excellence. And you are a hardworking volunteer.

Congratulations!

Rick

The Formula

Note: You could reverse the order here: start with congratulations and end with praise.

Beginning: Extend praise.
Middle: Expand on praise.
End: Offer congratulations.

The Makeover

Dear Birgit,

Your acceptance speech for the Business Woman of the Year award was graceful and witty. And you earned the recognition. As a meeting planner, you have a national reputation for excellence. As a hardworking volunteer, you are an asset to our community.

Congratulations!

Rick

Checklist

✓ Apply ego check. Start with *you* not *I*.

✓ Be empathetic. Goodwill letters need not be written at all, and that fact magnifies their impact. Handwriting them is especially thoughtful. And a correspondence card is particularly appropriate for a handwritten note. (See note on correspondence cards in the Checklist for #67.)

✓ Control verbs. Prefer active to passive verbs and replace *recognition is well deserved* with *you earned the recognition*.

✓ Monitor usage. Don't hyphenate *well deserved*.

✓ Use parallel construction to make your writing smoother. Follow *as a meeting planner* with *as a volunteer*—to use similar sentence structure to compare or contrast ideas.

Resources

WriteAssets Makeover Checklist

☐ Does my **first paragraph** hook the reader's attention and state my reason for writing?

☐ Have I used enough **empty space** to make the page inviting?

☐ Do my **headings and subheadings** outline and label ideas for readers who skim?

☐ Are my **main points** easy to spot and developed convincingly?

☐ Are **supporting ideas** relevant and organized effectively?

☐ Have I **telegraphed ideas** to busy readers—with well-designed typography and format?

☐ Do I use strong, active **verbs** that infuse my writing with energy?

☐ Do I include as many **transitional words and phrases** as are needed to keep the reader's mind from wandering?

☐ Are **spelling, capitalization, punctuation, usage, and style** internally consistent and correct?

☐ Is my **tone** diplomatic, positive, confident, and appropriately conversational or formal?

☐ Is my **language** free of jargon, pretension, prejudice, and ambiguity?

☐ Does my **last paragraph** tell the reader what our next steps will be or emphasize my main point?

☐ Do I empathize with the **reader's point of view** to make clear why I am writing and why the reader should be interested in what I have to say?

Author's Note: The WriteAssets Makeover Checklist and the WriteAssets Quick-Start Notes that follow it are based on handouts and overheads created for my corporate writing workshops.

WriteAssets Quick-Start Notes

To get started quickly on a makeover, answer the traditional five Ws (and an H):

WHO will read what I am about to write and what is their point of view?

WHAT do I want to accomplish?

 Check as many goals as apply:

☐   To get or take action.

☐   To provide information.

☐   To cultivate or give support.

☐   To promote goodwill. Specific information I need to include in the *first paragraph* to promote my goals includes

_____

_____

_____

WHAT are my main points? (List up to seven.)

 Possible key words: *issue, recommendation, conclusion, plan, proposal, overview, background, cost, problem, solution, cause, effect, goal, morale, perception, ethics, analysis, implications, change, participation, tradition, innovation, results, cons, pros, impact.*

1. _____

2. _____

3. _____

4. _____

5. _____

6. _____

7. _____

WHY should readers care about what I say?

Possible key words: *save, include, improve, help, streamline, gain, invest, promote, benefit, advantage, profit, cause, effect, environment, image, future, example, time.*

_____

_____

_____

WHERE are loose ends and how will I deal with them?

Possible problems: *inconsistency, contradictions, ambiguity, confusion, deficiency, unsoundness, irrelevancy, unspoken assumptions, negative impact, opposition, causes, effects, excessive risk, threatening or unfamiliar ideas.*

_____

_____

_____

WHEN will next steps occur and who will take them?

Dates and deadlines to include in *last paragraph*:

_____

_____

_____

HOW will I organize my ideas?

Outline your organizational scheme. (See Tactics for Organizing Ideas in this section.)

_____

_____

_____

Transitional Words and Phrases

Transitions, when properly handled, connect ideas, indicate relationships, and keep the reader's mind moving along with the writer's. A transition (made by a word, phrase, clause, sentence, or paragraph) provides a bridge for the reader between the idea that precedes it and the idea that follows it. Adding transitions is a quick fix for a makeover. (In the examples that follow, transitions are italicized, but they would not be in an actual business document.)

Transitions at Work

Without Transitions

The board of directors meeting was called to order at 2:30 P.M. No votes were taken. They lacked a quorum. The president asked the secretary to call board members and get a firm commitment to attend the next meeting.

With Transitions

The board of directors meeting was called to order at 2:30 P.M. *However*, no votes were taken *because* they lacked a quorum. *As a result*, the president asked the secretary to call board members and get a firm commitment to attend the next meeting.

Without Transitions

He closed his office door. He got a lot done. Everyone thought he closed the door to make telephone inquiries about a new job. He should have said he was going to close the door to finish writing a report that was due by noon.

With Transitions

He closed his door, *and* he got a lot done. *But* everyone thought he had closed the door to make telephone inquiries about a new job. *Of course*, he should have said he was going to close the door to finish writing a report that was due by noon.

Without Transitions

We hoped to avoid the expense of installing security cameras in our stores. A holdup man pointed a gun at the cashier in our Seventh Street branch last week and demanded all the money in the cash register. We've decided to install a security camera focused on the cash register in each of our stores.

With Transitions

We hoped to avoid the expense of installing security cameras in our stores. *Unfortunately,* a holdup man pointed a gun at the cashier in our Seventh Street branch last week and demanded all the money in the cash register. *In response,* we've decided to install a security camera focused on the cash register in each of our stores.

How Transitional Words Are Used

To amplify

Accordingly	In other words
Additionally	In the same way
Also	Moreover
Because	Similarly
Consequently	Simultaneously
Eventually	Specifically
For example	The next step
Formerly	What's more
Furthermore	Without dissension
In addition	

To continue

Again	In spite of
Also	Indeed
And	Meanwhile
Because	Of course
Even so	Simultaneously
Frequently	Sooner or later
Generally	Therefore
Granted	Ultimately
In some markets	Unfortunately

To contrast	
But	On the contrary
Despite	Otherwise
Even so	Rather than
However	Yet
In contrast	Unless
Nonetheless	

To emphasize	
Above all	Most important
Another key	Once again
As indicated	Under no circumstances
Beyond question	Without a doubt
In other words	

To conclude	
A final consideration	In other words
Accordingly	In short
As a result	In spite of
Cumulatively	In sum
In conclusion	Nevertheless
In consequence	The final effect
Inevitably	The implications
In the last analysis	Therefore

Author's Note: In the same or different form, part of this section on transitions—and of the next sections, Tactics for Organizing Ideas and One-Minute Grammar Review—first appeared in my book *Writing That Means Business*, published in 1984. The information is as useful today as it was then.

Tactics for Organizing Ideas

The tactics for organizing ideas discussed here apply to writing speeches and presentations as well as to letters, memos, proposals, and reports.

Logic

Decide whether your document will benefit most from deductive or inductive logic. *Deductive reasoning* moves from the general to the specific and is by its nature sound. *Inductive reasoning* moves from the specific to the general and may be sound or unsound. Deduction provides an airtight argument and is most often the best choice for a business document. But induction provides more interesting reading.

Deduction

Generalizations that form the basis for a logical conclusion: All A2Z computers use Ipswitch Basic. All Executive Micro computers are A2Zs.

Specific, Logical Conclusion: The Executive Micro uses Ipswitch Basic.

Induction

Specifics that form the basis for a logical conclusion: (A) Aeronautical, chemical, and electrical engineers have had to face, at various times recently, a softening job market in their respective fields. (B) With increasing frequency, companies seek engineers whose planning skills complement their technical skills. (C) Engineering schools have not been able to predict reliably, for entering students, which engineering specialists will be in demand when those students graduate.

General, Inductive Conclusion: Engineers are well advised to become both managers and technicians.

Organization Schemes

In addition to choosing the logic you will follow, select an organizational scheme for presenting information. Here are seven examples:

1. Chronological

You're moving your stock from one warehouse to another. You outline the sequence of events in the order in which they will occur, and you give any firm dates.

2. Geographical

The population in the country has shifted. You discuss the impact on your business area by area.

3. Hierarchical

You're writing a succession study. Proceed from the candidates for chief executive officer to those for chief operating officer to potential department heads.

4. Procedural

Your organization is upgrading its Internet connections. You enumerate the steps to be taken.

5. Level of Abstraction

General to Specific. You've recommended entering the fantasy-game market. You go from that generalization to an assessment of specific games you want your firm to produce.

Specific to General. You've come upon a new product that seems right for e-commerce. You work from a description of that product to a summary of the general requirements for your company's developing, marketing, and selling it at your Web site.

6. Importance

Most to Least Important. You're adding a new flavor to your line of soups. You assess the sources of supplies, starting with the most crucial ingredient and working down the list.

Least to Most Important. You have a public relations problem. You begin with the least alarming aspect and finally acknowledge something serious may have happened.

7. Cause and Effect

Cause to Effect. You've discovered a flaw in a supplier's copper tubing. You discuss the problems that have resulted from your company's use of that copper tubing.

Effect to Cause. Your atomic reactor has malfunctioned. You must explain what happened beginning with the nuclear accident.

One-Minute Grammar Review

PARTS OF A SENTENCE

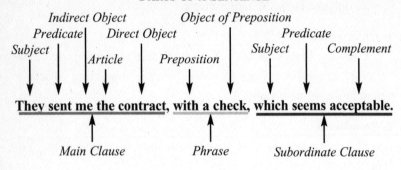

Indirect Object
Predicate | Direct Object | Object of Preposition
Subject | | Predicate
Article | Preposition | Subject | Complement

They sent me the contract, with a check, which seems acceptable.

Main Clause | Phrase | Subordinate Clause

PARTS OF SPEECH

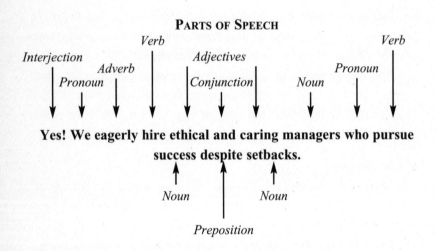

Interjection | Verb | Adjectives | Verb
Adverb | Conjunction | Pronoun
Pronoun | | Noun

Yes! We eagerly hire ethical and caring managers who pursue success despite setbacks.

Noun | Noun
Preposition

Jargon Generator

If you're ever at a loss for words, just pick an edgy adjective from both column A and column B and a trendy noun from column C. You'll get a phrase, which is as impressive as it is meaningless, that will position you as an expert—for example, a 1/11/5 (authoritative theoretical deconstructionist)—whom people will respect as beyond challenge.

A	B	C
1. authoritative	1. operationalized	1. application
2. componential	2. organizational	2. assessment
3. contextual	3. postmodern	3. benchmark
4. exponential	4. proactive	4. connectivity
5. foundational	5. process-oriented	5. deconstructionist
6. interactive	6. qualitative	6. demographics
7. mandated	7. reconfigured	7. facilitation
8. maximized	8. reengineered	8. framework
9. methodological	9. sociotechnologic	9. implementation
10. micromanaged	10. statistical	10. intervention
11. multidimensional	11. theoretical	11. meta-theory
12. nonhierarchical	12. triarchical	12. throughput

Author's Note: Similar versions of the Jargon Generator have appeared at my Web site (*www.writeassets.com*) and in overheads created for my corporate writing workshops.

Index

welcome to new customer,
254–56

D

damage control
for demotion, 157–59
for project, 155–56
dashes, 91
deductive reasoning, 266
defense of price increases, 248–50
dictated letters, 52

E

e-mail
announcing new Web site,
114–16
capitalization in, 156
cover letters via, 6–8
formal, 25
formatting, 8
tone for, 72, 120, 196
effect, use of, 131
ego checks, 5, 8, 23, 100, 120, 202,
213, 221, 229, 237, 241,
247, 250, 256, 258
emoticons, 196
employee stock ownership plan
(ESOP), 80–82
employees
acceptance of suggestion by,
92–93
alerts to, 46–47
benefits for temporary, 108–10
encouragement for improved
performance, 174–75
invitation to participate in company project by, 42–45
invitations to, 166–67
mediation program for, 89–91
notice to, of workshop, 36–38
persuasive letters for, 39–41
support for, with family crisis,

176–77
employer-assisted housing (EAH)
program, 83–84
empty space, 38, 45, 103, 131, 231
enclosures, 5
exclamation marks, 88, 196
explanation of error letter, 121–22

F

favor for peer, 240–41
formatting issues
in e-mails, 8
to emphasize key points, 65, 68,
96, 113, 116, 131, 141, 171,
177, 189, 200, 202, 207,
250, 256
empty space, 38, 45, 103, 131,
231
headings, 41, 45
italics, 38
lists, 25, 52, 68, 96, 131, 141,
231, 256
in memos, 84, 91

G

gerunds, 168–71
grammar issues
See also punctuation; word usage
capitalization, 7, 16, 41, 96,
146, 156, 165, 192, 231
contractions, 82, 88
dangling constructions, 25
hyphenation, xi, 5, 12, 27, 79,
141, 171, 218, 258
modifiers, 82, 86, 173, 213
prepositions, 23, 207
review of, 268
split infinitives, 113
subject-verb agreement, 38, 47,
98, 156, 171
verb tenses, 30, 103, 152, 175,
184, 217

merger announcement, 106–7
modifiers, 82, 86, 173, 213

N

negotiation, of job offers, 17–19
networking letter, 180–81
notices
    of budgetary constraints,
      168–71
    of changed credit terms, 111–13
    of colleague's illness, 224–25
    of employee benefit, 219–21
    staff workshop, 36–38
    status of recommendation,
      119–20
    travel schedule, 117–18
numbers, 162–63, 233

O

online ads, 6–8
organization schemes, 205, 265–67
outline style, 207

P

parallel construction, 38, 82, 100,
    258
perhaps, use of, 7
persuasive letters, 39–41
plus, usage of, 65
positive emphasis, 98, 107, 141,
    159, 221
postscripts (PS), 113
praise letters
    for annual report, 197–98
    for chapter president, 201–2
    for colleague, 195–96
    for a government service,
      193–94
    for subordinate, 226–27
prepositions, 23, 207
probably, use of, 7

problem resolution letters
    about bank errors, 60–62
    demand for invoice adjustment,
      56–59
procedures change memo, 94–96
projects, damage control for,
    155–56
promotions
    e-mail announcing, 85–86
    rejecting requests for, 26–27
pronouns, 159
proofreading, 27, 29, 38, 45, 55,
    100, 103, 127, 207, 229
proposal, 160–63
    request for, 66–68
public relations, 65, 72, 84, 103,
    105, 110, 116, 185, 250,
    253, 256
    internal, 91, 93, 152, 154, 171,
      221, 223
punctuation
    closing, 16
    colon, 10, 16
    commas, 10, 74, 91, 105, 107,
      118, 141, 152, 207, 225,
      229, 253
    dashes, 91
    exclamation marks, 88, 196
    with lists, 109
    quotation marks, 14, 47, 74, 215
    semicolons, 55
    slash marks, 12, 16, 68

Q

questions, 250
quick-start notes, 261–62
quotation marks, 14, 47, 74, 215

R

raises
    recommendations for, 31–32
    requests for, 28–30

About the Author

Hawley Roddick became a corporate writing consultant in 1984. Since then, she has designed and presented workshops and one-on-one coaching sessions for distinguished clients ranging from *Fortune* 500 companies to small nonprofit organizations. In addition, she acts as writer and editor for business clients. A Wellesley graduate, she is the author of three novels and two nonfiction books. She lives in Santa Barbara, California. Her Web site is *www.writeassets.com*

Photo by Gloria Betz